The "E" Is for Everything

Richard N. Katz,
Diana G. Oblinger, Editors

The "E" Is for Everything

E-Commerce, E-Business, and
E-Learning in Higher Education

EDUCAUSE
Leadership Strategies No. 2

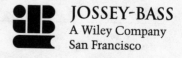

JOSSEY-BASS
A Wiley Company
San Francisco

This book is part of the Jossey-Bass Higher and Adult Education Series.

Jossey-Bass books and products are available through most bookstores. To contact Jossey-Bass directly, call (888) 378-2537, fax to (800) 605-2665, or visit our website at www.josseybass.com.

Substantial discounts on bulk quantities of Jossey-Bass books are available to corporations, professional associations, and other organizations. For details and discount information, contact the special sales department at Jossey-Bass.

 Manufactured in the United States of America on Lyons Falls Turin Book. This paper is acid-free and 100 percent totally chlorine-free.

Library of Congress Cataloging-in-Publication Data

The "E" is for everything: e-commerce, e-business, and e-learning in higher education / Richard N. Katz, Diana G. Oblinger, editors.—1st ed.
    p. cm.—(EDUCAUSE leadership strategies; no. 2)
Includes bibliographical references and index.
    ISBN 0-7879-5010-6 (pbk.)
    1. Universities and colleges—Computer networks—United States. 2. Internet (Computer network) in education—United States. 3. Universities and colleges—United States—Administration. I. Katz, Richard N. II. Oblinger, Diana G. III. Series.
    LB2395.7.E58 2000
    378'.00285'4678—dc21
                              00-008788

FIRST EDITION
PB Printing 10 9 8 7 6 5 4 3 2

The EDUCAUSE Leadership Strategies series addresses critical themes related to information technology that will shape higher education in the years to come. The series is intended to make a significant contribution to the knowledge academic leaders can draw upon to chart a course for their institutions into a technology-based future. Books in the series offer practical advice and guidelines to help campus leaders develop action plans to further that end. The series is developed by EDUCAUSE and published by Jossey-Bass. The sponsorship of PricewaterhouseCoopers LLP makes it possible for EDUCAUSE to distribute complimentary copies of books in the series to more than 1,700 EDUCAUSE member institutions, organizations, and corporations.

EDUCAUSE

EDUCAUSE is an international nonprofit association with offices in Boulder, Colorado, and Washington, D.C. The association is dedicated to helping shape and enable transformational change in higher education through the introduction, use, and management of information resources and technologies in teaching, learning, scholarship, research, and institutional management. EDUCAUSE activities include an educational program of conferences, workshops, seminars, and institutes; a variety of print and on-line publications; strategic/policy initiatives such as the National Learning Infrastructure Initiative and the Net@EDU program; a research and development program; and extensive Web-based information services.

EDUCAUSE

- provides professional development opportunities for those involved with planning for, managing, and using information technologies in colleges and universities
- seeks to influence policy by working with leaders in the education, corporate, and government sectors who have a stake in the transformation of higher education through information technologies
- enables the transfer of leading-edge approaches to information technology management and use that are developed and shared through EDUCAUSE policy and strategy initiatives
- provides a forum for dialogue between information resources professionals and campus leaders at all levels
- keeps members informed about information technology innovations, strategies, and practices that may affect their campuses, identifying and researching the most pressing issues

Current EDUCAUSE membership includes more than 1,700 campuses, organizations, and corporations. For up-to-date information about EDUCAUSE programs, initiatives, and services, visit the association's Web site at www.educause.edu, send e-mail to info@educause.edu, or call 303-449-4430.

PRICEWATERHOUSE COOPERS

PricewaterhouseCoopers is a leading provider of professional services to institutions of higher education, serving a full range of educational institutions—from small colleges to large public and private universities to educational companies.

PricewaterhouseCoopers (www.pwcglobal.com) draws on the knowledge and skills of 155,000 people in 150 countries to help clients solve complex business problems and measurably enhance their ability to build value, manage risk, and improve performance.

PricewaterhouseCoopers refers to the U.S. firm of PricewaterhouseCoopers LLP and other members of the worldwide PricewaterhouseCoopers organization.

Contents

List of Tables, Figures, and Exhibits

Tables

Figures

Preface

In September 2010, Jennifer S. walked onto the University of California Santa Cruz (UCSC) campus for the first time. She and her entering freshman classmates represented the first class of the Web generation—young people born with a silver mouse at their workstation. Few had known the world without the World Wide Web. Though new to the university, Jennifer had had numerous virtual tours of the campus. In fact, the campus's intelligent recruitment agent, Virtua-Slug, first contacted her over the Web in tenth grade as a result of her PSAT scores and a review of her electronic transcripts. Jennifer selected UCSC because of its academic reputation, redwood groves, proximity to the beach, and "safe distance" from her mother's home in San Francisco. It did not hurt that her two closest friends had also chosen UCSC. They would all be living in Crown College, one of UCSC's residential colleges.

Jennifer arrived at the campus having already completed two semesters of collegiate work, including an oceanography course taught at her high school by a member of the UCSC faculty. This course, which combined work on the Web with personal appearances by the professor, was offered in her junior year and factored heavily into Jennifer's decision to attend UCSC. Jennifer and Professor Stephens enjoyed corresponding during his office hours. She particularly enjoyed the atmospheric models he introduced her to and that she was able to download from the National Oceanographic and Atmospheric Administration to simulate a variety of ocean-based weather systems.

Although she was nervous in her freshman orientation, Jennifer smiled to herself as campus administrators and faculty described the Santa Cruz academic program. She wondered what it meant to be a "freshman" when at sixteen years old she already had met UCSC's core requirements and figured that she could start her environmental law program within three years.

Jennifer eagerly recorded the URL of the Santa Cruz class registration system on the personal digital assistant she had been issued, so that she could begin to select her fall courses. She also noted the address of the portal to the campus's consortium site where she could select among the on-line courses offered by thirty-five academic partners of the campus, including the seven other UC campuses, the California State University campuses, Stanford University, and several others. The campus had worked out all of the details to make it possible for her to cross-register at these institutions while still paying the fixed in-state fees.

Sitting beneath a stately redwood, Jennifer dialed into the campus network, thinking how well suited the campus was to the wireless technologies the university had implemented. She downloaded a variety of courses in earth studies, computational geochemistry, and oceanography and selected three classes on campus and one offered at Stanford. UCSC operated a shuttle bus to Stanford that would make it possible for Jennifer to alternate attending classes in Palo Alto with participation via the Web. She knew that she might not get all of these classes, but assumed that the complex expert systems and algorithms that would be used to review her credentials would be in her favor.

Later that day she received an e-mail message confirming three of her classes and wait-listing her for the fourth. In all, a good day! She and her high school friends met at the campus student center late that afternoon for cappuccino and to order their books. The virtual campus bookstore, Bay Tree Express, was linked to Amazon. com, her favorite site since childhood. She was mildly surprised to see that there were no required textbooks and ordered thirty of the less expensive required articles. After entering her debit card number, she sent off her order. She received an e-mail confirmation two minutes later and was advised that the articles ordered would be bound as three volumes, as she specified, and would be delivered to her dormitory by 10:00 A.M. the following day. The UCSC banana slug sweatshirts would arrive under separate cover at the same time and place.

Jennifer and her friends laughed and agreed that they now must officially be students. Despite feeling grown up, Jennifer was overcome by a wave of homesickness and made a mental note to send her mother an e-mail letter that evening. She would probably also send one to her father, who lived in Germany.

Preposterous? Yes, the scenario no doubt *understates* the likely student expectations and campus capabilities of a decade from now by an order of magnitude. In fact, the technologies that will be needed to support the capabilities described already exist in commercially tested form. Many of today's college-bound seven year olds have never lived without the World Wide Web. In 1998, 43 percent of all U.S. households operated at least one personal computer at home. Sixty-five percent of these households reported using educational software for their children at least once a month, and one U.S. household in four reported using on-line services regularly (Software and Information Industry Association, 1998). Home Internet access will likely reach the homes of all college-bound students in the United States well before 2010.

"E" is in the air. On nearly every billboard, in magazines, and in airports, an "e-revolution" is extolled. *Fortune* magazine columnist Stewart Alsop (1999) even proclaimed that the "e" in e-business will soon be irrelevant, meaning that this transformation will occur in the commercial sector so quickly that the only kinds of businesses that will survive will be e-businesses. He advises, "E or be eaten."

What is higher education to make of this widespread mania for and fascination with everything electronic? Is it just another (passing) management fad, or is something more fundamental and profound going on? If what is going on is indeed profound, and possibly transformational in nature, how will this e-revolution affect higher education? More important, how can higher education participate in the anticipated changes in ways that strengthen the best of what colleges and universities have accrued over the centuries?

These questions, and the issues that derive from them, are the topics that this book addresses. The chapter authors are united in the belief that the emergence of electronic and network-based services will in fact cut new channels through our myriad systems of education. The Internet and World Wide Web, which constitute the foundational infrastructure on which an electronic services revolution is being built, were developed and tested in university and research environments. The very openness of the Internet protocol (IP) standards on which the Internet rests is a reflection of higher education's need for open collaboration among disparately located scholars.

The issue for higher education is not whether student or faculty learning, communication, and socialization styles and proclivities will change, or whether college and university administrative services will migrate increasingly to electronic means. The preferences and styles of the members of higher education's multiple communities will evolve in part in reaction to broader changes occurring in the environments in which colleges and universities operate. Campus systems, services, and approaches will also change, because it will be increasingly difficult, costly, and isolationist to operate traditional services. Rather, the dominant issues facing the leaders of today's colleges and universities are what aspects to change and how fast can they be changed.

Jennifer's scenario is quite consciously campus based. In fact, we believe that the traditional and time-tested model of residentially based undergraduate education will continue to prosper. This mode of delivery continues to satisfy the needs of parents and students to foster learning and socialization and to acquire community-building skills. At the same time, it is important to note that this model today serves only 25 percent of the college-bound eighteen- to twenty-two-year-old population. It is also important to note that prosperity in this educational niche will not come to all and will be influenced by an institution's choices in coming to grips with the electronic services revolution. In particular, new providers will play an increasing role in the delivery of even traditional education and services, and new technologies will make it attractive for many existing institutions to extend their reach in pursuit of the globe's most promising students.

Time is of the essence. To partake of new bounties that will be available to colleges and universities in the knowledge-driven era— or for some, even to survive—profound and far-reaching commitments must be made quickly. These commitments must be made explicitly and publicly and must be accompanied by the investments of talent and funds that can make them real. This will be a challenge in environments long acculturated to deliberation and skepticism of fads and trends originating in industry.

The chapters in this book first penetrate through the hype and jargon that comprise much of the current popular dialogue and literature relating to electronic services and then identify the data, technical, and policy issues that must be addressed so that colleges and universities can begin to develop e-business strategies to move ahead in this important adventure.

The chapter authors agree that leadership, as always, lies at the heart of an organization's ability to realize the potential that new opportunities and challenges present. The electronic services revolution will require that leaders knit together campus services and organizations in ways that nearly defy imagination. No one ever claimed that change would be easy.

Boulder, Colorado   RICHARD N. KATZ
Chapel Hill, North Carolina   DIANA G. OBLINGER
March 2000

References

Alsop, S. "E or Be Eaten." *Fortune*, Nov. 8, 1999, pp. 85–87.

Software and Information Industry Association. "1998 Survey of Household Use of Information Technology." [www.siia.net/siia/default.htm]. 1998.

Acknowledgments

For those of us who have long advocated and championed a sea change precipitated by information networks, the time is now. The almost breathtaking speed of network development and the application of talent and imagination to the services delivered across networks is reshaping how businesses, governments, and cultural institutions perform their missions. This is an exciting time for us to lead, learn, and live.

We would like to thank our "net-generation" friends and colleagues for helping us challenge our assumptions and continue moving into the future. The contributors to this volume are some of the busiest, most thoughtful, and most respected opinion leaders in higher education. We are also indebted to a legion of professional colleagues who in the course of assembling this book have supplied an abundance of advice, insights, and critical feedback. Jim Dolgonas and Peggy Rogers, in particular, generously shared insights on approaches to Internet security being developed and deployed at the University of California.

We especially thank our students who never knew e-business couldn't be done!

This volume is part of the EDUCAUSE Leadership Strategies series. The creation and delivery of this series—and this volume—have been a team effort. EDUCAUSE president Brian L. Hawkins and the board of directors of EDUCAUSE have provided consistent support for this effort. Their enthusiasm is a real source of energy and inspiration. Our colleagues at PricewaterhouseCoopers have supplied more than the necessary financial support for each volume in this series. In fact, Jill Kidwell and her colleagues have shared the fruits of their experience in a variety of industries generously with us. Similarly, our colleagues at Jossey-Bass have been supportive in every way imaginable.

Every project of this kind needs a sparkplug, a conscience, and a taskmaster. We have been truly fortunate to work with Julia A. Rudy of EDUCAUSE. Julie's knowledge of, and passion for, the role played by information technology and resources in higher education is simply without peer. Every editorial process and product that she touches is immeasurably better for it.

R.N.K.
D.G.O.

The Authors

Kenneth C. Green is founder and director of The Campus Computing Project, the largest continuing study of the role of information technology in U.S. colleges and universities. The project is widely cited by campus officials and corporate executives as the definitive source for information about information technology issues affecting U.S. higher education. Green is also a visiting scholar at Claremont Graduate University of The Claremont Colleges, California. Author, coauthor, or editor of a dozen books and published research reports and more than three dozen articles in academic journals and professional publications, Green is frequently quoted on higher education, information technology, and labor market issues in *The New York Times*, *The Washington Post*, *The Los Angeles Times*, *The Chronicle of Higher Education*, and other print and broadcast media. He is an invited speaker at more than two dozen academic conferences and professional meetings each year. "Digital Tweed," Green's monthly column on information technology issues in higher education in *CONVERGE Magazine*, can be found at www.convergemag.com.

Richard N. Katz is vice president of EDUCAUSE, responsible for developing and delivering much of the association's educational program through international conferences, workshops, seminars, and institutes, as well as for member and corporate relations, research and development, and outreach. Prior to joining the association in 1996, Katz held a variety of management and executive positions spanning fourteen years at the University of California (UC). As executive director of business planning and practices, he was responsible for design and implementation of many of the nine-campus UC system's strategic management initiatives. At UC, Katz was awarded the Gurevich Prize and the Olsten Award and was the second recipient of that university's Award for Innovative Management and Leadership. He is author, coauthor, or editor of more than twenty books, monographs, and articles on a variety of management and technology topics. Katz received his B.S. degree from the University of Pittsburgh and his M.B.A. from the University of California at Los Angeles.

Jillinda J. Kidwell is a partner at PricewaterhouseCoopers (PwC) LLP, with ten years of consulting experience in strategy development, strategic repositioning, and restructuring for higher education and not-for-profit institutions. She has assisted large, research-intensive universities and their academic medical centers in responding to external and internal challenges. Her clients include Stanford University; Emory University; Washington University; the universities of Colorado, Pennsylvania, Maryland, Minnesota, Missouri, and Illinois; the California State University System; and the San Diego, Santa Cruz, and San Francisco campuses of the University of California, among others. Kidwell is the author of many publications on administrative restructuring in universities, and she is a frequent speaker at the conference of the National Association of College and University Business Officers, the Forum for the Future of Higher Education, and PwC's CEO Roundtable. Kidwell received her B.A. from Calvin College and her M.B.A. from Tulane University.

John Mattie serves as partner in charge of PricewaterhouseCooper's Education and Healthcare Industry Global Risk Management Solutions group, which provides risk management and control solutions in business process and information technology for educational and health care organizations. With over twenty years of experience, Mattie has served as client partner to Yale University and Stanford University and is currently client partner for Assumption College, Babson College, MIT, Worcester Polytechnic Institute, the University of Chicago (internal audit), and the University of Missouri (internal audit). He presented at the annual meeting of the Eastern Association of College and University Business Officers on new reporting standards for higher education and at the annual meeting of the National Association of College and University Business Officers (NACUBO). Mattie helped write NACUBO's debt management handbook and assisted in the development of PwC's Internal Control Questionnaire and Financial Reporting Checklist for Education Institutions. He received his B.S. degree in accounting from the University of Hartford.

Diana G. Oblinger is vice president for information resources and chief information officer for the sixteen-campus University of North Carolina (UNC) system. At UNC, Oblinger oversees strategic planning and policy development for technologies that support the university's instructional, research, and public service activities and facilitates collaborative approaches to system-level technology issues. Previously she held several management positions within IBM in academic programs and strategy, academic consulting, and solution development for instruction, and was IBM director of the Institute for Academic Technology. Prior to joining IBM, Oblinger was on the faculty at the University of Missouri and at Michigan State University. She is internationally known for her thought leadership in distributed learning, technology, and the future of higher education. Oblinger is coauthor or coeditor of four books and more than two dozen monographs and articles. She received her B.S., M.S., and Ph.D. degrees from Iowa State University in botany and cytogenetics.

Michael Sousa is a principal consultant in the education/not-for-profit consulting practice of PricewaterhouseCoopers LLP. He has more than nine years of experience in consulting to colleges and universities in the areas of e-business, strategic planning, business process redesign, and project management. He has worked with Princeton University, the University of Massachusetts, the University of North Carolina, the University of Connecticut, and Stanford University, among others. Prior to joining Coopers & Lybrand LLP, Sousa was assistant to the senior vice president at Boston University for five years. He holds a B.S. degree from Boston College's Carroll School of Management and an M.B.A. degree from Boston University's School of Management.

Robert A. Wallhaus is a higher education consultant whose clients have included state systems of higher education, the National Center for Educational Statistics, and individual colleges and universities. He has served on numerous federal advisory panels and has provided leadership in professional organizations, serving a term as president of the Association for Institutional Research. Early in his career he served on the faculty of the University of Illinois in the mechanical and industrial engineering department and was director of research, then deputy director at the National Center for Higher Education Management Systems (NCHEMS). From 1978 through 1995 he worked for the Illinois Board of Higher Education, where he was responsible for reviewing and approving academic programs, supervising a professional staff who carried out analytical studies and formulated policy, and making budget recommendations to the governor and legislature. He received his Ph.D. in industrial engineering with an emphasis in operations research from the University of Illinois.

David L. Wasley is assistant to the associate vice president of information resources and communications at the University of California (UC) Office of the President. Wasley's work focuses on infrastructure planning broadly across the university. UC is in the beginning phases of deploying universal digital credentials for all members of the university community, an activity that is seen as the cornerstone for the development of middleware services and deployment of next-generation technologies within the university and in support of electronic commerce with external partners. Wasley is active in university and national venues that are developing common vision and standards in these areas.

Navigating the Sea of "E"

Diana G. Oblinger, Richard N. Katz

In a networked world, you can add an "e-" to almost anything: e-mail, e-commerce, e-business, e-procurement, e-tailing, e-government, e-learning. In the business community, the Internet and the World Wide Web are fundamentally changing the way many companies operate: promoting brands, selling products, communicating with customers, and managing suppliers. In government, these technologies are changing how payments are made, grant proposals are submitted, patents are filed, and services are provided. In education, the Internet and Web are changing instruction, research, administration, and public service. Student services professionals are rethinking what information is provided to students and how, as well as the decision-making tools that add value to that information. Purchasing, library services, and financial processes are being transformed as an evolving set of technologies is adapted to the needs of colleges and universities. Perhaps most striking is how this collection of capabilities, from e-mail to collaboration to knowledge management, is changing the expectations of our society.

In this evolving environment, there are many new household names—eBay, Amazon.com, America Online (AOL), and many others. More significant than the names of the latest players is the new set of dynamics that is emerging:

- The network economy thrives on speed, flexibility, and the relentless pursuit of innovation.

- Large organizations consolidate and small ones proliferate to balance scale, efficiency, and innovation.

- The delivery of value and market responsiveness are replacing traditional decisions as the basis for allocating resources.

- Lower-priced or higher-quality offerings do not automatically confer competitive advantage (International Business Machines, 1999).

Adrift in the Sea of "E"

Educational policymakers and information technologists may share a confusion over the growing—and undisciplined—evolution of language to describe what is known variously as e-business, e-commerce, and so forth. Indeed, although the addition of the "e" prefix to any word seems to add value in both private capital markets and advertising, higher education readers are wise to take a somewhat skeptical view. In fact, *e-business* has become a generic term signifying all manner of electronic operations.

In general, the term *e-business* refers to the application of a variety of information technologies to the delivery of an organization's mission. In particular, e-business assumes the application of Internet, extranets, intranets, and the World Wide Web to an organization's processes and delivery systems. Increasingly e-business assumes the integration of these technologies with a variety of related technologies (data warehousing, data mining, intelligent agents, and so forth) to replace physical processes with new processes that can be accomplished over networks. Some even think of e-business as an evolutionary step that reflects a progression of capabilities from on-line catalogues and electronic payments at the earliest stages of effort, to the adoption of so-called personalization technologies and supply-chain integration at later stages. Industry analysts and pundits are advising that ultimately (and perhaps soon) this ubiquitous e-prefixing of every human activity will abate as the majority of enterprises accomplish this integration and replacement of technologies and processes and as "e-business" becomes indistinguishable from business. This mainstreaming of e-business has two important implications:

1. It is not critical, or perhaps even helpful, to master the jargon of this important trend.

2. The trend itself, and in particular its application at the enterprise (for example, college or university) level, is likely to become a matter of extraordinary importance.

Despite our reservations about this jargon, the addition of the "e" prefix is a useful and efficient shorthand for a complex variety of technologies and activities. For this reason, and due to the popularity of this convention, the chapter authors use a variety of related terms, especially *e-commerce, e-business,* and *e-learning.*

E-business is used as the generic and overarching term signifying all manner of internal and external operations and processes conducted over networks. In general, e-business also assumes the use of the World Wide Web as an infrastructure for "doing business" (for example, identifying goods or services, selecting a desired product, ordering a product, and in some cases actually delivering the product). The dominant idea of e-business is that an organization "gains an advantage by being able to serve customers wherever they happen to be—in a store, on the phone, on-line, or offline" (Alsop, 1999, p. 87).

E-commerce is used typically to describe transactions (not all economic in nature) between one individual or organization and another. It is "the marketing, sales, and payment for goods, services and experiences using electronic means" (Norris and Olson, 1999).

There are a growing number of enterprise Web sites where businesses market, sell, and support products.

E-commerce companies are focused on Internet-based sales, whether business-to-business or on-line retailing to consumers. Of these, some are aggregators bringing diverse brands to market (for example, Amazon.com). Others provide an electronic market for industry buyers and sellers, such as MetalSite and ChemExchange and retail auction firms such as eBay. A third type of e-commerce company enables buyer-driven commerce such as Priceline.com (International Business Machines, 1999).

Although $23 billion was spent in on-line merchandise in 1998, e-commerce between businesses was five times greater than the consumer market. Business-to-business e-commerce is exploding. Shifting business to the Web is straightforward and more cost-effective. Forrester Research predicts that in 2003, business-to-business e-commerce will reach $1.08 trillion, a thirty-five-fold increase from 1998.

A substantial amount of on-line commerce already is associated with colleges and universities. The research firm Student Monitor estimates that students will spend $700 million in on-line purchases in the year 2000. By 2002 it expects on-line spending by college students to exceed $14 billion. In addition, alumni and athletic fans purchase sweatshirts, caps, and other college logo products over the Web ("Wired on Campus E-Life," 1999).

E-learning is a rapidly expanding category of e-business. Defined as using the Internet for instruction in postsecondary education and training (Baer, 1999), the prospects for e-learning appear to be tremendous. Digital technologies for distance—or distributed—education have applications for children, college or university students, corporate learners, and those seeking personal enrichment. The combined effects of increased demand and enabling technologies are creating a significant market for distance education. International Data Corporation expects a compound annual growth rate of 33.1 percent over the next several years, predicting that demand will increase from 5 percent of all students in higher education institutions in 1998 to 15 percent by 2002 (Rochester, Boggs, and Lau, 1998).

Myriad new products, services, and providers are entering the e-learning "marketspace." For example, curriculum and content development is being provided by university spin-offs such as OnlineLearning.net, NYU Online, and educational publishers. Content development is linked to companies that provide software learning environments (for example, Lotus, Convene, WebCT, Blackboard, and Eduprise.com). Teleconferencing firms are being integrated into the learning delivery systems (for example, Caliber, One-Touch). Educational management organizations (for example, UNEXT.com or University of Phoenix) are attempting to span the range of traditional university functions.

Related to e-learning, content service companies and enterprise Web sites create or provide information that can be obtained online (International Business Machines, 1999). These include firms that organize content created by others (for example, Yahoo) and "destination" sites that provide specialized content (for example, Weather.com). Typical business models are based on advertising revenues or related product sales, but some information is also sold directly (for example, WSJ Interactive).

The content area for higher education presents significant potential. The Gartner Group (1998) expects a dramatic increase in the content that will be delivered electronically to students. Estimates are that 60 percent of students will access content electronically by 2003.

Other terms for describing network-based transactions have also become popular, though they generally will not be used in this book.

E-procurement describes the use of network, Web, database, and related information technologies for paperless procurement. E-procurement can range from using electronic data interchange (EDI) to digitally processed transactions to sophisticated order management and inventory control systems. Electronic payments reduce paperwork and cut costs. The Federal Reserve estimates the overall cost of check writing to the U.S. economy is $44 billion a year in paperwork, processing, and labor (Donahue, 1998).

Using another form of e-procurement, some institutions have begun to allow authorized staff members to order goods up to a certain value (for example, $5,000) on a purchasing card, which eliminates approximately 80 percent of traditional purchase transactions (Finlayson, 1999). An emerging benefit of e-procurement, beyond reducing paperwork, is that it allows organizations to compare prices and services more effectively. Over the Web, the number of price comparisons can be virtually unlimited and instantaneous. For example, "shopping bots" such as RUSure and MySimon can be used to scour the Web to identify purchasing alternatives and compare prices. New companies are emerging to provide institutional and individual customers with these technical capabilities and the benefits of pooled purchasing power.

E-care is a term that some use to refer to using the Web to deliver information, support, services, and decision-making aids to individuals inside or outside an organization. In higher education, electronic student services is the most common form of e-care. For example, the New York University (NYU) Book Centers are simplifying the process of identifying, locating, and purchasing books for NYU's forty-six thousand students. An interactive Web site allows students to enter their student identification number or a particular course number from their computer to generate a complete list of the books needed for their courses. Students can also learn whether certain books are in stock as well as how many copies are available and where each is located across the four book centers.

Many e-care sites offer features designed to serve people, such as the ability to read through lists of frequently asked questions or to send a query via e-mail. Such sites capitalize on the fact that most people tend to ask the same questions over and over (the repeat rate often runs from 50 to 70 percent). Analysts estimate that a telephone inquiry costs twenty-five to thirty dollars; serving that same individual over the Web costs just two to three dollars (Clague, 1999).

E-care in higher education can also apply to employees (for example, enrolling for a health care plan). Other functionality that a human resource site can offer includes opportunities to access or update personal information; enroll for benefits, training, and deductions; review lists of internal job postings; process time cards; or access employee handbooks (Savage, 1997).

E-access refers to the sale of network connections or network management services (portals) by Internet service providers (ISPs). These business models are typically based on monthly subscription fees. Some portals, such as AOL and GeoCities, strive to build online communities. Access fees are predicted to drop; many companies intend to move to more sustainable models based on advertising and transaction shares (International Business Machines, 1999). This has already begun in higher education with the introduction of Campus Pipeline, MyBytes.com, Jenzabar.com, and others.

Benefits of E-Business

One of the reasons for moving to e-business is that such a move allows, or even forces, organizations to innovate. The business model behind Amazon.com is fundamentally different from that of traditional booksellers, for example. For other organizations, the rationale focuses on efficiency and effectiveness. Focusing the attention of higher education on innovation (as well as on efficiency and effectiveness) is a promising change strategy that builds on the traditional propensity of college and university faculty and staff to create and innovate.

The returns on investment (ROIs) from internal or e-business are positive. For publishing applications, the estimated ROI is 21 percent. For order management, collaboration, commerce, and customer service, the ROIs range between 40 and 50 percent. Inventory management applications exceed a 50 percent ROI. These returns, as always, will be hard to translate into higher education environments, where quality is often defined in terms of student-faculty ratios. However, an e-business infrastructure creates the early

opportunity to lower the costs of delivering institutional services
and over the longer term makes it possible to extend the reach of
the institution in ways that do not always add costs. Real revenue
increases and cost reductions are possible.

In multiple facets of college and university operations, an effective e-business strategy can play an important role and provide
valuable benefits. First, the cost of operations and services can be
reduced. Applications often can be processed more efficiently on-
line than manually. By saving costs, educational resources can be
freed up and applied to other priority programs. Second, the quality of services can be improved. For example, course or job listings
that are maintained electronically can be kept up to date more easily. Students can avoid spending time trying to register for classes
that are already full or applying for jobs that are no longer available.
Finally, the coordination and communication between offices can
be enhanced, speeding up work flow and decision making.

Implications of E-Business

E-business only accents the reasons for institutions to continue their
investments in networking. Being "wired" has become a competitive edge in today's society. Many students are selecting universities
based on how wired they are. In part, this is because students are
performing more functions on-line, from registering for classes and
communicating with professors to ordering take-out food.

Internet commerce shifts the balance of power to the buyer. On
the Net, competition is just a click away. If people have trouble finding a book at Amazon.com, they can go to barnesandnoble.com.
People can easily find a wealth of price comparison information on
the Net. CompareNet, for instance, offers detailed information
on more than 100,000 consumer products. The Net allows consumers and corporate buyers from all over the world to band together
and pool their purchasing power, leveraging volume discounts
(Hof, 1999). This tendency to shift power is heralded by some as
the emergence of the exchange economy. This shift presents col-

leges and universities with an important potential source of cost savings and poses new challenges to these institutions as they move to deliver (and price) their own services over networks.

There are a number of implications of e-business dynamics that will affect higher education as well as business and government:

- The use of the network for e-business can dramatically reduce transaction costs. In a bank, it costs roughly a dollar to do a transaction in a branch, fifty cents over the phone, twenty-five cents through an ATM, and thirteen cents over the Internet.

- The network can reduce barriers to entry. The landscape is altered significantly when a competitor can enter your market with an 87 percent reduction in distribution costs (Gerstner, 1998).

- The network enables the low-cost reproduction and distribution of information-based offerings. A value proposition based predominantly on information may be insufficient in the future. Mass customization and the addition of value may be required.

- Networks readily cross traditional departmental, industry, and national boundaries, broadening markets and increasing competition.

Among the fundamentals of e-business are rethinking goals, organizational structures, funding, technology, and collaboration. If we accept the premise that traditional rules may not translate into success in an e-business environment, applying existing institutional models to this new environment is risky.

References

Alsop, S. "E or Be Eaten." *Fortune*, Nov. 8, 1999, pp. 85–87.

Baer, W. S. "E-Learning: A Catalyst for Competition in Higher Education." *iMP Information Impacts Magazine*, June 1999. [www.cisp.org/imp/june_99/06baer.htm].

Clague, M. "Understanding E-Business." In D. Oblinger and R. Katz (eds.), *Renewing Administration: Preparing Colleges and Universities for the 21st Century.* Bolton, Mass.: Anker, 1999.

Donahue, S. "Government Writes First Echeck." *Wired,* Jul. 1, 1998.

Finlayson, M. "Rethinking 'Rethinking Administration': A Cautionary Tale." In D. Oblinger and R. Katz (eds.), *Renewing Administration: Preparing Colleges and Universities for the 21st Century.* Bolton, Mass.: Anker, 1999.

Gartner Group. "Higher Education Scenario." Presentation at the Gartner Group Symposium, ITxpo98, Lake Buena Vista, Fla., Oct. 12–16, 1998.

Gerstner, L. V. Unpublished remarks made at the Organization for Economic Cooperation and Development Ministerial Conference, Ottawa, Canada, Oct. 8, 1998.

Hof, R. D. "What Every CEO Needs to Know About Electronic Business: A Survival Guide." *Business Week,* Mar. 22, 1999, pp. EB9–EB49.

International Business Machines. "Global Market Trends." Unpublished internal report, 1999.

Norris, D., and Olson, M. *What Every Educator Needs to Know About E-Commerce: Building Competencies for Tomorrow's Opportunities.* Washington, D.C.: National Association of College and University Business Officers, 1999.

Rochester, J., Boggs, R., and Lau, S. *On-line Distance Learning Becoming More Popular Way to Learn.* IDCFlash W17781. Framingham, Mass.: International Data Corporation, Dec. 1998. [www.idc.com].

Savage, M. "HR: Focusing on Strategic Business Issues and Automating or Eliminating the 'Routine Administrivia.'" Unpublished paper, 1997.

"Wired on Campus E-Life." *USA Today,* Aug. 19, 1999, pp. B1–B2.

2

First to the Ballroom,
Late to the Dance Floor

Kenneth C. Green

For students entering or returning to college in the fall of 1999, the back-to-college buying experience was decidedly different from years past. Early market research data from several sources suggest that a small but significant number of students ordered textbooks, computers, dorm furnishings, and other products from the rising tide of "dot com" companies that focus exclusively on the college market. Indeed, a quick scan of magazine, television, and campus newspaper ads targeting college students during summer and fall 1999 reveals that books, clothing, travel services, music, computers, and a wide array of other products and services were readily available and aggressively promoted to students by traditional retailers as well as start-up companies, all doing business on the Internet.

Consequently, it is probably appropriate to point to fall 1999 as the moment when significant numbers of students, like significant numbers of consumers in general, began doing serious commerce

Data reported in this chapter are from The Campus Computing Project's 1999 Campus Computing Survey. Begun in 1990, The Campus Computing Project (www.campuscomputing.net) is the largest continuing study of information technology in U.S. higher education. The 1999 Campus Computing Survey report is based on data provided by chief information officers and other senior campus information technology officials at 530 two- and four-year public and private colleges and universities across the United States.

over the Internet. Indeed, press reports leading into the 1999 Christmas buying season were rife with references to wired holiday shoppers. For example, nine weeks before Christmas 1999, *Business Week* reported that holiday "e-sales are expected to explode to $12 billion, almost triple [1998's] tally" ("The Great Yule Tide Shakeout," 1999). Concurrently, a steady stream of reports in other business media, including *Forbes, Fortune, The Industry Standard*, and *The Wall Street Journal*, confirmed that 1999 was the year when Internet and Web-based enterprise-to-enterprise sales and services captured significant attention and significant dollars in industry and corporations.

Yet U.S. colleges and universities themselves were conspicuously absent from the 1999 explosion in e-commerce. The very institutions that helped to build the ballroom (that is, the Internet) have been coming late to the dance floor to do business there. Compared to other sectors of the economy, colleges and universities, serving a highly wired population of students and faculty, have been slow to embrace and build for e-commerce.

Survey Results

New data from The Campus Computing Project's annual survey on information technology planning and policy issues reveal that comparatively few institutions had e-commerce capacity as school opened in the fall of 1999 (Green, 1999). Without question, two- and four-year colleges and universities across the United States (and, for that matter, around the world) have embraced the Internet and the World Wide Web as a tremendous resource for compiling and disseminating information. However, the vast majority of U.S. colleges have not begun to engage in a wide range of Web-based activities that would support the educational experiences and opportunities of their students through access to content and other resources, provide significant convenience and more and better services to students, and improve various aspects of the enterprise-to-enterprise or supply-chain business activities that are common to organizations of similar size and complexity.

Perhaps the best single indicator documenting the absence of e-commerce capacity in higher education comes from a comparison of the kinds of services that colleges and universities currently offer on their campus Web sites. As Table 2.1 shows, less than a tenth of the institutions participating in the 1999 Campus Computing Survey reported e-commerce capacity over their Web sites as campuses welcomed students back to school in 1999. In contrast, admissions services (undergraduate application, college viewbook, and so forth) were commonly available on institutional home pages across almost all sectors of the campus community.

Aggregating across the twenty-one different kinds of Web-based services (for example, admissions, financial aid, course registration, library catalogue, course reserves, on-line courses, faculty directory, athletic event schedules, alumni services, and press releases) that the 1999 Campus Computing Survey tracked, it is clear that the most common Web-based services involve the passive or minimally

Table 2.1. Services on the Campus Web Site, Fall 1999 (percentages)

	Undergraduate Admissions Application	Financial Aid Application	Library Card Catalogue	On-line Courses	E-Commerce
All institutions	70.2	34.1	74.6	45.6	8.4
Public universities	85.1	56.7	97.0	74.6	22.4
Private universities	81.5	29.6	96.3	40.7	3.7
Public four-year colleges	77.2	36.8	86.8	60.5	11.4
Private four-year colleges	76.4	30.9	80.9	25.8	5.6
Community colleges	48.1	28.2	53.4	49.6	3.8

Source: Green, 1999.

interactive display of information (for example, student application forms, faculty and staff directory, course listings, and library catalogues). Web applications that require more sophisticated programming, controls, and support (such as course registration and sales) are much less common across all sectors of higher education.

The absence of such capacity on college and university Web sites is only one indicator of how institutions are (and *are not*) planning for the arrival of e-commerce. Indeed, the 1999 Campus Computing Survey also reveals just how few colleges and universities are doing such planning. As Table 2.2 shows, less than 5 percent of the nation's two- and four-year colleges and universities have a strategic plan for e-commerce, and less than a fifth are developing such a plan. Although there are some variations in planning activity across sectors, the percentage of institutions that report a current strategic plan for e-commerce is consistently low, regardless of the type of institution.

Table 2.2. Strategic and Financial Planning for Information Technology, Fall 1999 (percentages)

	Strategic Plan for Information Technology	Financial Plan for Information Technology	Have an E-Commerce Plan	Developing an E-Commerce Plan
All institutions	61.0	44.3	4.3	17.3
Public universities	60.6	27.3	3.0	28.8
Private universities	61.5	42.3	3.9	26.9
Public four-year colleges	65.2	43.0	3.6	18.0
Private four-year colleges	61.6	55.2	4.7	12.3
Community colleges	58.7	39.7	4.8	15.1

Source: Green, 1999.

These data are not necessarily surprising. Indeed, through the 1990s, colleges and universities were slow to develop their strategic plans for information technology (IT) overall, let alone true financial plans that provide both a plan and the money to acquire and retire aging computers, outdated software, and other IT resources (Green, 1997; Green and Jenkins, 1998).

Consistent with the absence of planning for e-commerce is the low rating that campus officials give to their institution's current capacity for e-commerce as part of the broad institutional technology infrastructure (see Table 2.3). It is not surprising that data networks earn a very high rating from the survey respondents. After all, campus networks have been the focus of institutional IT planning efforts and financial investments for more than a decade. In contrast, e-commerce is a recent arrival on the technology agenda. Moreover, similar to the experience in some parts of the corporate sector, colleges and universities have perhaps been slow to embrace e-commerce because most senior officials do not fully understand

Table 2.3. Rating the Campus IT Infrastructure, Fall 1999

	Computer and Data Networks	User Support Services	On-line Resources in Library	Web Resources for Instruction	E-Commerce Capacity
All institutions	5.7	4.8	5.3	4.6	2.8
Public universities	6.0	4.8	5.4	4.9	3.4
Private universities	6.0	5.2	5.8	5.2	3.0
Public four-year colleges	5.7	4.9	5.4	4.8	3.0
Private four-year colleges	5.7	4.8	5.3	4.6	2.5
Community colleges	5.5	4.7	5.1	4.6	2.8

Note: Mean scores; 1 = poor, 7 = excellent.
Source: Green, 1999.

its significance and how it supports the mission of the organization and facilitates many enterprise-to-enterprise operations. An additional factor in higher education, which is also true of some businesses and industries, is that internal e-commerce advocates such as chief technology officers may not hold a vice-presidential position and thus may not be part of some of the formal (and equally important informal) conversations about long-term strategy and objectives.

However, some evidence suggests that e-commerce has yet to emerge as a significant strategic issue for many institutions (perhaps the majority of them). While not denying the importance of other issues that compete for time and resources in the campus IT strategy, Tables 2.4 and 2.5 reveal that e-commerce is not yet a first-tier IT priority for most institutions. Table 2.4 shows that e-commerce gets a midrange ranking compared to other IT issues and priorities

Table 2.4. Strategic Issues and Concerns for Colleges and Universities

	Helping IT Staff Stay Current	Retaining IT Personnel	Developing Budget Model for Equipment	Using Web Resources in Instruction	E-Commerce
All institutions	6.2	6.2	6.0	6.0	4.2
Public universities	6.2	6.5	5.9	6.3	4.9
Private universities	6.3	6.2	5.4	5.9	4.9
Public four-year colleges	6.1	6.2	6.1	6.2	4.4
Private four-year colleges	6.2	6.2	6.1	5.9	3.7
Community colleges	5.7	6.0	6.2	6.0	4.1

Note: Mean scores; 1 = not important, 7 = very important.
Source: Green, 1999.

confronting senior campus IT officials. Table 2.5 suggests that campus officials view e-commerce as a function and service that resides on the horizon rather than a pressing issue that demands immediate attention and implementation.

Taken in aggregate, the data from the 1999 Campus Computing Survey suggest that e-commerce is an arriving issue rather than a current and pressing priority in institutional IT planning and strategy. Thus, while e-commerce explodes in consumer and enterprise markets, planning and implementation will be much slower in the campus community.

Why So Slow to Dance?

What explains the apparent chasm in perspectives and prioritieson e-commerce issues and strategy that separates campuses and corporations? Part of the difference can be attributed to organizational and campus culture issues and the lingering divide between

Table 2.5. Issues Affecting Campus IT Planning, 2000–2003

	Network Security	Internet2	Wireless Networks	Internet Video- conferencing	E-Commerce
All institutions	6.4	4.4	4.3	5.1	4.5
Public universities	6.6	5.9	4.8	5.8	5.2
Private universities	6.3	5.4	5.2	5.3	5.2
Public four-year colleges	6.5	4.5	4.4	5.1	5.0
Private four-year colleges	6.4	3.8	4.0	4.7	4.2
Community colleges	6.3	4.2	3.9	5.2	4.2

Note: Mean scores; 1 = not important, 7 = very important.
Source: Green, 1999.

academic and administrative computing. Where does the responsibility for e-commerce reside: Academic computing? Administrative computing? The college business office? In this context, planning for e-commerce is a complex undertaking because IT responsibilities on campus are more dispersed than in business and industry; no one campus official or single campus office has the ultimate responsibility and authority for the wide range of IT and financial issues that e-commerce involves.

In addition, the actual implementation of e-commerce is no small challenge. Ultimately most institutions (like most corporations) will buy rather than build an e-commerce solution. Early reports from campuses engaged in e-commerce implementation suggest it is a timely and costly process: twelve to eighteen months invested in planning plus actual dollar costs that can easily approach (if not surpass) $5 million for a consumer- and enterprise-oriented system.

Moreover, while corporations may view e-commerce as critical to operations and survival, many campus officials do not view it as urgent for their institution and thus may be less willing to make the required investment of people, time, and money. These campus officials are conscious of competing claims for such resources and remain less certain of the immediate e-commerce benefits. Unfortunately, traditional return-on-investment models are not necessarily appropriate for assessing e-commerce in a campus environment, because the benefits are not precisely measured in terms of increased sales and administrative savings, metrics that readily apply to business and industry. Rather, in service organizations such as colleges and universities, doing business electronically can improve the quality of services to clients (students) and the efficiency of interactions with product and service providers. However, it will not necessarily save money according to traditional measurements.

The transaction costs that financial institutions charge for using credit cards are also a concern for many campuses, especially public institutions. While retail businesses (including college bookstores) have incorporated these transaction costs—roughly 1.5 to 2.5 percent of the sale of a product or service—into pricing, colleges and universities remain largely cash businesses that process checks rather than credit cards. Understandably, campus officials are hesitant to surrender 1.5 or 2.0 percent of student tuition payments, a significant sum of revenue, to the banks that might provide processing services for credit cards. But over time, these transaction costs will be similar to other (structural) costs that colleges and universities have to incur as credit cards become the preferred form of payment for growing numbers of students and their families, who prefer both the convenience and the benefits of credit cards (the extra float on the payment, the frequent flyer miles).

Yet the transaction and related costs associated with e-commerce may be offset by other institutional benefits, such as reduced personnel costs for processing payments and faster access to funds. Certainly the growing use of "smart cards" on many college campuses, both public and private, suggests that initial implementation and recurring transaction costs are manageable.

Too, the rigidity of the campus calendar poses important challenges to any conversations about the rapid deployment of e-commerce on college campuses. Most colleges and universities have a seven-week window, from July 7 to August 15 each year, for implementing major changes in IT systems and resources: new computers in faculty offices, new administrative software, and so forth. (The rigidity of the campus calendar is antithetical to the core concepts of continuous quality improvement.) Because e-commerce implementation involves a wide array of campus systems and campus offices (libraries, bookstores, finance, admissions, financial aid, and purchasing, among others), the window for its planning and implementation becomes all the more challenging.

Summary

Without question, electronic commerce looms large as a critical strategic and IT issue for all sectors of higher education. For the campus community, e-commerce involves far more than the capacity of campus Web sites to process application fees from prospective students or to accept credit card payments from alumni who want logo clothing from the college bookstore.

In the final analysis, e-commerce on campus is about the *institutional mission*. It involves a wide range of consumer and enterprise services that both support the academic mission of the institution (for example, on-line access to content) and enhance core administrative functions and services. However, the early data profiling e-commerce on campus reveal that colleges and universities have been conspicuously absent in the current explosion of such activity in the United States. Compared to other sectors of the economy, colleges and universities, serving a highly wired population of students and faculty, have been slow to embrace and to build for electronic commerce. Institutions and campus officials will have to do more, do better, and do it soon.

References

"The Great Yule Tide Shakeout." *Business Week*, Nov. 1, 1999.

Green, K. C. *Campus Computing, 1997: The National Study of Information Technology in American Higher Education*. Encino, Calif.: The Campus Computing Project, 1997.

Green, K. C. *Campus Computing, 1999: The National Study of Information Technology in American Higher Education*. Encino, Calif.: The Campus Computing Project, 1999.

Green, K. C., and Jenkins, R. "IT Financial Planning 101." *NACUBO Business Officer*, Mar. 1998.

3

E-Learning

From Institutions to Providers, from Students to Learners

Robert A. Wallhaus

E-learning—technology-based education—will change how we count things in higher education. It will bring about a need for new kinds of data to support both policy analyses and management and administrative functions. New analytical conventions will be needed to gain insights about instructional costs, faculty work, and student participation. And new approaches for collecting data, from both learners and learning providers, will need to be developed. At the same time, traditional modes of learning will continue to be offered, so new measures will need to be compatible with traditional measures of the learning experience.

This chapter is based on the work of the National Postsecondary Education Cooperative Policy Panel on Technology, chaired by Virginia McMillan, executive vice president of the Illinois Community College Board, and a working group established to implement the panel's directions, cochaired by Dennis Jones, president of the National Center for Higher Education Management Systems, and Sally Johnstone, program director at the Western Interstate Commission for Higher Education. The chapter author served as consultant to both the panel and the working group.

How E-Learning Will Affect College and University Operations

Expanded use of computer and network technologies to deliver instruction and provide access to information resources has the potential to change higher education significantly: its organizational relationships, financial operations, student participation patterns, and faculty roles and responsibilities. The use of such technologies will result in the removal of time and place constraints, with instruction available when the learner wants it and at a virtually unlimited number of locations. E-learning will open a wider range of student choices, resulting in a transformation from an institutional-centered context for the delivery of instruction to a learner-centered emphasis. There will be greater competition and specialization across a wider range of educational providers, and at the same time a greater need for providers to cooperate and share resources.

These developments will have far-reaching ramifications for higher education administration and for the data that are needed to support policy development and decision making. To set future directions in postsecondary data systems that will be responsive to the new world of e-learning, we must first examine how e-learning will affect college and university operations, organizational configurations, faculty roles and work, student participation patterns, and revenue and expenditure flows.

New Institutional and Programmatic Configurations

E-learning will bring about many changes in higher education. Students, who historically have come to learning sites, increasingly will participate at locations remote from the campus and the instructor. Rather than being affiliated with a single institution, they will be associated concurrently with multiple providers and modes of instruction. Educational services will become unbundled, with different providers carrying out various functions: curricular development, delivery of instructional modules, provision of student services, student evaluation, and awarding of credentials. Students will assume greater control over their educational experiences by designing programs that fit their specific needs with regard to program content, length, delivery mode, and location. Program completion will be defined increasingly by the knowledge gained and skills mastered rather than credit hours earned.

Table 3.1 contrasts institutional and programmatic configurations associated with conventional approaches to the delivery of instruction with configurations made possible through computer and network technologies. In fact, the table overstates the differences; many hybrids of the configurations have existed for some time.

These new organizational and programmatic configurations raise many questions that affect data systems:

- How will unbundled functions be described and aggregated to understand the cost, process, and results of serving students?

- How will irregular instructional patterns be measured?

- What new data collection methodologies will be needed to capture data about multiple learning sites and providers?

- Because traditional campuses and delivery modes will continue to exist, how will state and national data systems accommodate many different types of institutional structures and characteristics?

New Faculty Roles and Work Patterns

Faculty responsibilities and workloads will undoubtedly change as faculty become involved in technology-based delivery and instructional support systems. Less emphasis will be placed on lecturing and greater emphasis on facilitating the educational process—for example, by providing learning assistance in time patterns and modes tailored to the needs of individual students. Efforts will be made to draw on the capabilities of technology to increase student learning productivity by integrating technologies in ways that are

Table 3.1. Conventional Instructional Delivery Versus E-Learning

Conventional Instructional Delivery	E-Learning
Students physically come to learning sites (campuses).	Students participate at locations remote from the instructor.
Students take classes at times predetermined by the institution.	Learner determines when to access instruction based on individual needs.
Single college or university provides all instructional and student services needed by students.	Educational services are unbundled, with different providers developing course materials, delivering instruction, evaluating students, awarding credentials, providing access to information, and offering various student services.
Student is affiliated with one institution at a time.	Learners are concurrently associated with multiple providers and modes of instruction.
Learning objectives are specified by the institution.	Learners shop for opportunities that fit their specific needs.
Terms of the relationship with students are determined by the institution (for example, time and place of instruction, sequences of courses, terms of admission).	Students design their own program with regard to content, length, structure, and so forth.
Program completion is defined by the institution in terms of credit hours earned.	Program completion is defined by knowledge gained and skills mastered.

tailored to the optimal learning modes of individual students. It is also possible to capitalize on the flexibility of technologies to make better use of student time and to make faculty content and delivery specialists available to students independent of location. Faculty will be learning facilitators, intervening when needed and selectively providing motivation and assistance to students. Faculty will find it easier and more compelling to collaborate; increasingly they will work with multiple providers and institutions, team with other faculty, and make specialized contributions in skill and knowledge areas as well as in instructional functions (for example, courseware development).

These new roles and patterns of faculty work will have data system ramifications, resulting in questions such as the following:

- What new definitions of faculty activities will be needed to capture the full scope of faculty contributions?

- How will faculty productivity be measured (for example, what workload measures will be used to capture what an instructor does when responding to student questions as they arise via e-mail or interacting with students using a listserv)?

- How will faculty load and compensation be determined as faculty contribute simultaneously to multiple institutions at multiple locations?

Analyzing Student Participation Patterns

Student participation patterns have become more complex as larger numbers of older, nontraditional students have pursued higher education goals. Many students no longer follow linear, lockstep paths through a well-defined educational program. Rather, they simultaneously pursue educational and training experiences with multiple providers, and many work at paid employment at the same time. Noncollegiate providers are playing an increasingly important role in delivering training and providing credentials. Expanded use of technology will accelerate these trends, and the need to address related data and analytical issues will likely become more pressing. Asynchronous modes of learning made possible by computer-based systems and the Internet raise questions with regard to when learning begins and how long it lasts. Asynchronous learning opportunities shift the focus in the direction of student goals and highlight the fact that they are not always synonymous with such institutionally defined goals as degree completion.

As technology results in multiple providers and modes of delivery, it will become more difficult to learn about student participation by seeking information from institutions. New ways will need to be found to link student data across providers, some of which may not be traditional institutions and learning modes. Self-paced, asynchronous experiences also tend to undermine the utility of time-based proxies for student participation and outcomes (for example, retention and graduation rates, enrollment census dates) and also have implications for the awarding and portability of credentials. Furthermore, many administrative operations depend on traditional student attendance measures, including assessment of student charges, unit cost analyses, administration of student financial aid, recording student progress, budget formulas, and determining eligibility for professional licenses. How can traditional institutional-based data collection systems be linked to student-based data collection systems? How can "old" data points be mapped to "new" data points so valid trend analyses and comparative analyses can still be carried out?

Assessment of Student Progress and Learning Gains

A wider array of providers and a more market-oriented environment will place a higher premium on information about the quality of learning experiences in consumer choice, accountability, and regulatory contexts. However, measuring student progress depends on having insights regarding what sort of progress is being measured and toward what end. With technology, students to an even greater extent will determine their own learning goals and will be the source of information about those goals. They will proceed toward learning goals at different paces and with different rhythms, which will be impossible to capture with traditional measures of "seat time" as the principal indicators of student progress. Competency-based measures will likely become increasingly important as the basis of academic accounting.

Analysts have historically encountered challenges in studying the relationships of input, environmental, and outcome variables, but the simultaneous delivery of multiple learning experiences by multiple providers using multiple delivery systems will add new complexity to studies of the effects of inputs and environment on learning gains. Electronic instructional delivery systems provide opportunities to capture timely data about student behaviors, learning strategies, and patterns of achievement, but they also heighten concerns about confidentiality and privacy with respect to student data. Issues related to privacy and confidentiality will be exacerbated by the ease with which vast amounts of data can be captured and accessed using technology.

Analysis of Revenue and Expenditure Streams

E-learning will prompt new categories of costs or a shift in the relative importance of certain costs. For example, courseware development, help desk services for faculty and students, remodeling and rewiring facilities, expanding access to computers and software, and electronic storage and transmittal of information are becoming significant objects of expenditure for colleges and universities. Although current accounting systems appear capable of accommodating revenues and expenditures related to technology-based systems, difficulties could be encountered in reconciling revenues and expenditures across the fund accounting procedures used in higher education with the charts of accounts and accounting procedures used by noncollegiate providers of instruction and student services. Time frames will be more important in an e-learning environment because e-learning will change the life cycle of assets. For example, the shorter time frames for obsolescence that are generally associated with technological resources will need to be addressed in determining depreciation schedules and classifying capital and operating expenditures.

Procedures for allocating expenditures and revenues across multiple providers pose some troublesome questions:

- How are student tuition and fees collected from multiple sites that are supported by different providers and staffed by faculty from different institutions to be distributed?

- What proportion of the costs of shared facilities, faculty, and equipment will be paid by the various providers?

- How will revenues and expenditures for shared and unbundled operations be reported, and by whom?

- What are the ramifications of these allocation decisions for student financial aid awards?

Similarly, new student and faculty activities may require new classification structures and definitions or clarification as to how they are classified in current program structures (for example, is responding to student questions via e-mail a support activity or a direct instructional activity?). Since new electronic modes of delivery will need to coexist with traditional instructional delivery across higher education, accounting and reporting systems will need to be designed to accommodate multiple delivery systems simultaneously.

A Conceptual Framework for Examining Data System Requirements

A broader context for describing the learning process is needed to capture the new organization configurations, more complex student participation patterns, changing faculty roles, and new revenue and expenditure flows. This conceptual framework has been developed by a working group of the National Postsecondary Education Cooperative (NPEC, 1999) that is examining the data ramifications of e-learning. This framework can be used to develop key data system components describing learners and learning providers and, most important, the relationships among these components. This framework thus becomes the basis for developing data system directions at the state and federal levels that are responsive to the changes brought about by the widespread adoption of e-learning, and consequently has implications for campus-based data systems as well.

The conceptual framework defines learners very broadly to mean individuals involved in the advancement of skills or knowledge. The term *learning provider* includes not only the traditional postsecondary institutions but nonpostsecondary providers and new kinds of providers that are emerging with the expanded use of technology, such as developers of Internet-based courseware.

A learning experience can involve an individual learner working independently with a single learning provider, or multiple learners as well as multiple and different types of providers. For example, instruction could be delivered over the Internet, employing interactive multimedia learning materials developed by a commercial vendor (provider 1); facilitated by a faculty member from a university that sponsors the course or module (provider 2); with learning results assessed using a standardized test administered by a testing service (provider 3); and credit awarded by the different colleges and universities whose students are availing themselves of the learning experience (providers 4). Learning may occur simultaneously at multiple sites and in regular or asynchronous patterns.

A conceptual framework that captures the full scope of possible learning experiences and interactions between learners and learning providers is based on the components of a classification structure displayed in the appendix of this chapter. Fully understanding the learning experience not only requires information about learners and providers as reflected in this structure; it also requires an ability to analyze the relationships between learners and providers and between the various subcomponents of learners and providers. For example, Exhibit 3.1 describes the relationship between provider functions and provider resources. The cells of this matrix could contain a description of these relationships in terms of a measure or analytic convention. For example, the use of faculty in curriculum development, information delivery, or facilitating and tutoring

Exhibit 3.1. Relationships Between Provider Functions and Provider Resources

Provider Resources	Provider Functions						
	Developing Curricula	Accessing Information Resources	Delivering Information	Facilitating/ Tutoring	Providing Student Services	Assessing Learning	Credentialing
Faculty							
Facilitators							
Product developers							
Technicians							
Technology							
Licenses							
Facilities							

could be measured in full-time equivalents (FTE). In addition to using faculty (measured in FTE), information delivery could use technicians (measured in clock hours), technologies (measured in hours or dollars), and facilities (measured in square feet).

Many other relationships between learners and providers and the subcomponents of learners and providers could be developed. For example, Table 3.2 shows the relationship between learner participation patterns and information delivery mechanisms. Traditionally, student credit hours and contact hours have been used to describe this relationship, and these measures are appropriate for face-to-face-instruction and regularly scheduled (synchronous) participation patterns. However, these traditional measures do not adequately describe asynchronous participation patterns in which learners choose different schedules for, and durations of, their learning experiences. In some instances, no feasible relationship exists between learner participation patterns and provider delivery mechanisms; for example,

Table 3.2. Provider Delivery Mechanisms in Relation to Learner Participation Patterns

Learner Participation Patterns	Synchronous	Asynchronous
Face-to-face instruction (lecture, seminar)	X	
Laboratory	X	X
Work based (clinical, apprenticeships)	X	X
Print		X
Audio	X	X
One-way audio-video	X	
Two-way audio-video	X	
Two-way audio–one-way video (for example, satellite)	X	
Computer based, self-paced		X
Computer based, regularly scheduled	X	

it would be difficult to support two-way audio-video delivery in an asynchronous mode cost-effectively.

Theoretically, a relationship could be defined between any combinations of the subcomponents of learners and providers. In fact, any combination of the subcomponents of the taxonomy shown in the appendix could constitute a relationship that would be important to capture in higher education surveys or studies. Nevertheless, some of these relationships will be more meaningful and useful than others in an administrative, policy, or analytical context. The NPEC working group examined these relationships in developing the priorities and recommendations on higher education data systems that are presented in the following section.

Developing New Data Definitions and Analytical Conventions

Several challenges become readily apparent in a consideration of which components of the taxonomies of learners and learning providers will be most affected by e-learning. First, much of the new information that seems to be important will be very difficult to obtain from institutions. Instead, data about learner access to e-learning, participation patterns, and learner goals and outcomes can be provided only by students. Second, the pace of change in e-learning, in such areas as technology-based delivery modes, will necessitate frequent updates to definitions and analytical conventions. And the turnaround times currently associated with institution-based surveys are simply not responsive to the dynamics of e-learning. Different judgments will be made about the priorities of new kinds of information and modifications to current postsecondary data systems as e-learning applications evolve. Table 3.3 summarizes areas that will likely be most affected in the immediate future.

The first broad area, learner participation, focuses on data that would generally need to be obtained from students. The second set of data issues, concerning technology-based delivery, involves data

Table 3.3. Taxonomy Areas Most Affected by E-Learning

Data Concerning Learner Participation
- Measures of learner participation
- Learner participation patterns and interaction with providers
- Learner access to technology
- Learner outcomes
- Learner goals

Data Concerning Delivery of E-Learning
- Provider prices
- Provider resources
- Expenditures associated with the use of technology faculty
- Provider geography in relation to delivery mode
- Delivery modes related to technology
- Functions of providers related to technology resources
- Provider characteristics in relation to provider functions

that are generally collected from postsecondary providers. In some cases, the direction for modifying or supplementing postsecondary data systems is relatively straightforward; in other areas, a feasible approach to obtaining important new data is not at all clear. The following sections discuss the data system ramifications of each of the components and relationships across the taxonomies of learners and learning providers.

Data Concerning Learner Participation

The first broad area, learner participation, focuses on data that would generally need to be obtained from students: measures of learner participation, learner participation patterns (interaction with providers), learner access to technology (including the extent to which learners have access to and use technology and the barriers to that use), and learner outcomes and goals.

When learners provide information about how they interact with technology in the learning process, their responses depend on how technology is defined, and this is where the first set of challenges is encountered. The 1999 Adult Learner Survey and the Postsecondary Quick Information System (National Center for Education Statistics, 1997) defined technology in terms of specific delivery systems (for example, interactive audio-video, television and radio, satellite, e-mail, the World Wide Web, videoconferencing). A problem in describing technology in terms of specific delivery modes and media is that definitions and classifications tend to become obsolete, thus undermining trend analysis. Using broader classifications such as "computer based" and "network based" provides a greater likelihood of tracking the dynamics of technology use across time. But although generic definitions better support analyses of trends in the use of technology, they sacrifice information about the mix of different technologies that are being deployed at any point in time. An option is to combine the strengths of both approaches by using the generic questions in regularly scheduled surveys over time, supplemented by periodic special studies that focus on specific types of technology that are in use at any given time. Similar approaches could be used in collecting data from providers about e-learning.

Measures of Learner Participation

Probably the most fundamental data about higher education relate to how many students are participating and to what extent they are participating. This information is used in many ways: in resource allocation and budgeting processes at all levels of higher education, setting admissions targets, and decisions about institutional and program capacity.

Traditionally student participation has been measured in enrollment counts and credit hours. The debates about which students to count (for example, credit versus noncredit), when to count them (for example, opening fall or annual), and how to measure the intensity of participation (for example, full-time versus part-time

counts, or full-time-equivalent conventions) reflect many complexities. These complexities will surely be exacerbated by wider
adoption of different modes of e-learning, for two primary reasons.
First, learners will more frequently be simultaneously involved in multiple learning experiences with multiple providers; and, second,
technology will facilitate self-paced and self-scheduled learning
(that is, asynchronous learning).

The first question that must be addressed with regard to learner
participation is "participation in what?" That is, what constitutes a
learning experience? The Adult Learner Survey uses a very broad definition of *learning experience:* "different kinds of education and training programs, courses, workshops, and seminars" delivered for credit
as well as not for credit and by postsecondary providers as well as by
providers that do not have primarily a postsecondary mission. This
broad definition is feasible when samples of learners are interviewed.
It is virtually impossible to implement uniformly in institutionally
based surveys across the full scope of postsecondary learning experiences and providers.

For the immediate future, it will probably be necessary to focus
on formally organized learning experiences when providers are the
source of data. Stated pragmatically, the unit of analysis will need
to be the "course" and the participation measure "course enrollments." Increases in simultaneous student participation in multiple
institutions will make it more difficult to obtain unduplicated counts
at higher levels within the postsecondary hierarchy. At the state
level, this will require a unit record student tracking system, which
many states are implementing or have implemented for at least
some of their institutions (Russell, 1995). At the federal level, it
will require a comprehensive national student tracking system,
which is not going to be established in the foreseeable future. At
the campus level, institutions will face greater difficulties in keep-
ing track of enrollments as they support multiple sites through
e-learning and as "their students" move from one provider to another.

Measuring Interaction Between Learners and Providers

Interactions between learners and providers will require different measures for different modes of delivery and for fixed schedules versus variable schedules. Traditionally, clock hours or credit hours have been used. These measures continue to be relevant for regularly scheduled learning experiences, whether these are through e-learning or face-to-face contact with instructors. Options for measuring learner-provider interactions include credit hours, clock hours per day or week, incidence (times per day or week), percentage of day or week spent in a learning activity, and number of courses per term or year.

Credit hours may be applicable for most asynchronous learning experiences and clock hours for both credit and noncredit offerings. However, it is difficult to see how a single metric will be applicable to all types of learner-provider interactions that are possible with e-learning. The following modes of participation seem to be important:

1. Type of credentialing
   - Credit, leading to a credential
   - Credit, not leading to a credential
   - Noncredit
2. Type of provider
   - Postsecondary providers
   - Nonpostsecondary providers
3. Delivery media (see Table 3.2)
   - Computer based (site-specific computer based, Internet based)
   - Interactive audio-video based
   - Face to face
   - Laboratory
   - Work based

4. Pattern of delivery
   - Synchronous
   - Asynchronous

If one conceives of a matrix with multiple dimensions reflecting these modes of learner-provider interaction, appropriate measures could be assigned to each cell, providing a comprehensive, albeit complex, picture of how learning is being delivered. These same categories could also be used in collecting and analyzing data about instructional delivery when the focus is on learning providers.

Learner Access to Technology

A policy concern at all levels within higher education centers on the extent to which learners are effectively capitalizing on e-learning opportunities. The following broad areas in which opportunities could be enhanced (or, conversely, in which barriers could be removed) could be used in learner surveys and special studies. (Some of these specific subcategories will likely change as technology changes.)

1. Access to technology
   - Access to computers
   - Access to the Internet
   - Access to interactive audio-video sites
   - Reducing the costs associated with technology
2. Readiness to use technology
   - Better understanding of technology
   - Raising interest in using technology
   - Better training in the use of technology
   - Removing apprehensions regarding the use of technology
3. Effectiveness of technology in the learning process
   - Reducing concerns about the impersonal characteristics of technology

- Removing concerns about the quality of instruction delivered using technology

Learner Outcomes and Goals

From a data definition perspective, learner goals and learner outcomes differ primarily in that goals are specified prior to the learning experience, while outcomes are generally determined after the learning experience. Higher education has long struggled with the definitional, analytical, and measurement issues related to student outcomes. E-learning will heighten the importance of addressing these issues in two significant ways.

First, e-learning provides students a greater opportunity to pursue a wider variety of student-defined goals. Students will not be constrained to develop levels of skills and knowledge that are institutionally defined and packaged in prescribed programs. This means that student outcomes will need to be defined in ways that are consistent with student goals, and, perhaps more important, information about student goals and outcomes will need to be obtained directly from students. This does not imply, however, that outcomes defined from an institutional perspective will become less important; it simply adds another dimension to data systems.

Second, it may be possible to overcome some of the problems of measuring participation and learner-provider interaction by turning to measuring learner outcomes. Participation measures are currently used as proxies for outcomes in many policy development and decision-making contexts. In the long run, it may be easier, and even necessary, to look beyond time-on-task metrics to measuring outcomes and competencies, particularly in the case of asynchronous delivery modes.

Many efforts have been made to define the outcomes of higher education, often from different perspectives or to support different policy purposes. A good point of departure for data system development related to goals and outcomes is a taxonomy that Patrick Terenzini (1997) developed, drawing on historical work.

Data Concerning Delivery of E-Learning

The data system definitions, analytical conventions, and design issues addressed in this section concern data that would generally be available from postsecondary providers. Of course, the first-order questions are what constitutes a postsecondary provider and what universe of providers would be the object of a given survey or study. E-learning will invite participation of a wider range of nontraditional providers, many of whom will focus on a narrower number of functions than the full set of services commonly offered by residential colleges and universities. Defining what *provider* means is not in itself so difficult; the difficulty lies in maintaining comparability and data compatibility across a widening range of different kinds of providers.

Student Charges, Discounts, and Technology Requirements

Colleges and universities have begun to institute special student charges and discounts related to technology and requirements related to student ownership of computers. The Campus Computing Project survey addresses a wide range of policies related to the use of computers on campus, including fees and requirements concerning computer ownership (Green, 1998). The difficulty in this area is in capturing the specifics of the wide range of practices that have already evolved. It will likely be necessary to use broad, generic definitions in statewide and national surveys that are interested in tracking student charges, discounts, and requirements related to the use of technology.

Expenditures Associated with the Use of Technology

New kinds of expenditures associated with e-learning will be significant and therefore will need to be separately identified in data

systems at all levels within higher education. It will be important
to develop common definitions of expenditure categories to achieve
comparability of financial reporting across institutions. The following broad categories seem to encompass the full scope of new kinds
of expenditures associated with e-learning:

- Infrastructure (for example, bandwidth, facilities)

- Equipment (for example, computers, routers)

- Software (for example, operating system, application)

- Student-faculty support (for example, training,
  help desk)

- Content (for example, courseware development or
  acquisition)

One trade-off consideration is how much detail is to be captured
within each of these broad categories. Obviously data about specific computers will lose utility over short periods of time. But is it
meaningful to aggregate expenditures across all types of computational equipment? It depends to a large extent on how the data are
to be used.

Another difficult set of questions revolves around where e-learning expenditures are classified and reported organizationally and pro-
grammatically—for example:

- Are infrastructure expenditures assigned to the larger
  category of physical plant expenditures?

- Are student-faculty support costs classified with
  campuswide institutional support expenditures?

- Are what we have called content expenditures associated with individual academic units, while equipment
  and software expenditures are assigned across both
  campuswide and academic and administrative units?

In addressing these questions, we must keep in mind that all expenditures associated with e-learning are not technology expenditures (direct faculty expenditures in most cases will continue to be larger than technology costs), and not all technology expenditures will necessarily be associated with e-learning. These issues are related to costing procedures.

Finally, it will be necessary to determine how to handle depreciation of equipment and infrastructure costs, and particularly how to treat the time frames associated with obsolescence of technology. Traditionally colleges and universities have classified expenditures that reoccur over short periods of time as operating expenditures, and one-time expenditures in such areas as facilities that would be useful over long periods of time are classified as capital expenditures. Depreciation schedules for capital expenditures allowed them to be annualized over projected periods of service. The short time frames associated with the obsolescence of technology-related expenditures raise the questions about how to apply traditional conventions, such as the following:

- Are expenditures for remodeling and equipping interactive audio-video classrooms capital expenditures?

- What is the useful life of today's interactive classrooms?

- Would it be appropriate to use general obligation bonds to support such construction or remodeling?

Provider Geography in Relation to Delivery Mode

Colleges and universities typically keep track of and analyze where their students come from (in-district and out-of-district, in-state and out-of-state, county, or school district) for admissions and marketing purposes, and, in the case of public institutions, to assess tuition. With e-learning, the flip-side question will be increasingly important: Where is the institution going geographically to reach students?

Because technology will extend the geographical reach of colleges and universities, the possible sites served and geographical categories that are of potential interest will be virtually unlimited, from in-district sites to foreign countries. Fundamental questions that need to be answered include these:

- What categories of sites will be tracked?

- What measures will be used to capture participation at the different sites?

- What delivery mode is being used to serve learners at different geographical sites?

Expanded Faculty Activities Resulting from Technology

E-learning will likely have a significant impact on faculty work. To some degree, the changes will simply reflect a shift in emphasis across the activities currently used in the National Study of Postsecondary Faculty, which collects data about faculty work in the areas of teaching by level of instruction, research and scholarship, professional growth, administration, service, and outside consulting or freelance work (National Center for Education Statistics, 1999). However, additional categories of faculty activity will need to be defined or elevated in the aggregation conventions used to analyze faculty work. The taxonomy of the instruction function in the appendix shows how the NPEC working group viewed these shifts in emphasis. The National Study of Postsecondary Faculty asks respondents to report the percentage of time spent in each of these broad areas of activity. Percentage time will continue to be a useful metric for tracking changes in faculty work and responsibilities.

Functions of Providers Related to Technology Resources

The taxonomy in the chapter appendix identifies the following array of functions that could be carried out by learning providers: instruction, research, public service, academic support, institutional support, operation and maintenance of physical plant, and auxiliary enterprises. At this level of aggregation, these categories look like the primary and support classifications that have long been used to describe the functions of colleges and universities. However, as subcategories are developed, particularly in the instructional area, it will be necessary to add new functions that will be important in e-learning (see the taxonomy in the chapter appendix).

It will also be important to link functions to other components of the taxonomies of learners and learning providers. Instructional costing procedures, for example, involve distributing faculty and other resource measures across the activities (instructional functions) identified in the appendix. Resource measures must then be converted to expenditures, and costs per learner participation measure calculated. Usually the costs of support functions such as advising and assessing are allocated to primary instructional functions to which learner participation measures are directly linked (for example, delivery of information). Of course, the distribution and allocation conventions are dependent on selecting a unit of analysis, such as a course. And a common student participation measure must be chosen, or separate unit costs must be developed for different modes of instruction.

Other relationships that would be important are between functions and delivery mode, delivery media, and learning outcomes. Functions will also serve to define specialized providers.

Characteristics of Learning Providers Related to the Adoption of Technology

Traditionally, postsecondary institutions have been defined in terms of control (public, private, and proprietary) and mission (the emphasis placed on research, public service, and levels and programs of instruction). These descriptors will continue to be useful in describing colleges and universities. However, as new organizational configurations emerge, driven at least in part by e-learning, the traditional descriptors will not be adequate to characterize these new types of learning providers.

This evolution of new organization configurations seems to be simultaneously moving in two different directions. On one hand, cooperative arrangements, such as regional consortia, are springing up across the country; on the other hand, specialized providers are taking on functions normally carried out by comprehensive colleges and universities, such as curriculum (courseware) development. In an attempt to describe institutions that are capitalizing on computer- and telecommunications-based technologies, Wolf and Johnstone (1999) have developed a taxonomy based on such factors as organizational relationships, role in certification, and how students are served. The taxonomy has the following elements:

- Virtual university

- Virtual university consortium

- Academic services consortium

- University information consortium

- Virtual program

- Virtual certification institution

- Traditional accredited institution with electronic courses

To the extent that specialization and unbundling occur, provider descriptions and provider functions will tend to become synonymous (for example, virtual certification institutions in the above list). In fact it will be useful to characterize providers by selectively drawing on different components of the taxonomy of learning providers, including mission (postsecondary and nonpostsecondary), control, organizational configuration (for example, consortium), and types of programs offered.

Unbundling and multiorganizational configurations pose significant problems in accountability, consumer protection, and quality assurance contexts. Indeed, accrediting bodies and states with licensing and consumer protection responsibilities are grappling with jurisdictional problems created by specialized learning providers and virtual delivery modes that span state and regional boundaries. At this point, we have scant experience with and understanding of the educational outcomes associated with e-learning, adding a further complication to accountability, consumer protection, and quality assurance processes.

Pitfalls and Breakthroughs, Challenges and Opportunities

In the early 1960s, computer-based data systems made it possible to use records and files efficiently over and over again, and for multiple purposes. Data from payroll, admissions and registration, and accounting processes could be aggregated and linked in ways that could support planning, decision making, and analytical studies. States and the federal government built their information systems on these aggregations of institutional records; these systems, such as the Integrated Postsecondary Education Data System (IPEDS), continue to provide the preponderance of data that are used for planning, analysis, and accountability. Although institutionally derived aggregate data will continue to find utility for planning and management purposes, these data systems were not designed to support those purposes.

In the 1970s, some leading institutions began to invest in data systems designed to support planning, management, and analysis (such as faculty activity and assignment analyses), not operational purposes. And by the mid-1980s, the low costs of huge amounts of high-speed computer storage made it possible to contemplate the development of student unit record systems. High school feedback systems, enrollment tracking systems, and student follow-up systems are examples of what could be called student transition data systems, because they generally capture data at points where students move from one experience to another—from secondary to post-secondary education, from one college or university to another, and between education and work. Student unit record systems are characterized by the significantly expanded analytical flexibility they offer as contrasted with aggregations of institutional data.

Higher education is not alone in capitalizing on the low cost of high-speed computer storage; business, governmental, and social service agencies and consumer and financial service organizations have also developed unit record systems. We are beginning to recognize that there is some overlap between the files of these many noncollegiate organizations and the records maintained by higher education institutions, and that these organizations have information about potential, current, and former students that would be quite useful for planning and policy development. A prime example of such systems is the matching of graduation data with unemployment insurance records to gain insights concerning the employment of postsecondary graduates. The possibilities of linking information about postsecondary students across the large numbers of unit record files maintained by nonpostsecondary organizations heighten concerns about privacy and confidentiality, and well they should. These systems are characterized by the fact that they are not dependent on postsecondary institutions as a source of data. In fact, they raise the possibility that employers and nonpostsecondary organizations will be an important source of data for colleges and universities.

Irregular patterns of student participation and the growth of off-campus markets for training and education are turning students into the primary unit of analysis and source of data, trends that will accelerate with e-learning. Postsecondary education will need to turn to student and general population surveys as an important source of data. Student- and population-based surveys offer advantages beyond the insights and analytical flexibility they provide. They can alleviate confidentiality concerns because institutions will not be the source of these data and participating students need not be identified and can simultaneously give permission for institutions to use their responses for analytical purposes.

E-learning will result in the many challenges noted throughout this chapter. But it will also provide the means for addressing many of these challenges. For example, the World Wide Web will be used to collect and edit data, and data can be obtained on-line from students when computers are used as an integral part of the learning process. Instructional management systems will become an integral part of e-learning courseware. These systems are capable of capturing detailed data during the learning process, including how much time students spend on different parts of the course, the extent that they are understanding certain material, and the types of learning processes that lead to better progress for individual students. These are precisely the data concerning asynchronous learning that are difficult to derive from institutional data systems. Instructional management systems can be thought of as mini–student records systems. And therein lies a potential serious difficulty for institutions as they acquire courseware that has been developed independently on campus as well as by other institutions, consortia, and commercial vendors: institutions could end up with literally hundreds of incompatible student records systems.

E-learning will result in many challenges for data systems designers and users—pitfalls and breakthroughs, challenges and opportunities—to be sure.

Appendix

Classification Structure Describing Learning Providers

Characteristics
- Organizational descriptors
  - Control (public; private, nonprofit; private, for profit)
  - Mission
    - Title IV eligible
      - Carnegie classifications

Primarily postsecondary education (PSE) mission
Primarily non-PSE mission (business,
government, social service)
Informal
- Organizational configuration
  - Single institution
  - Multiple institutions—for example, consortia
- Programs (level and content—for example, Classification
  of Instructional Programs [CIP])
- Accreditations

Functions

- Instruction
  - Developing curricula
    Defining content (level and CIP)
    Identifying information
    Organizing content and information (packaging
    courses, modules)
    Developing courseware
    Developing curricular resources
  - Accessing information resources
  - Delivering information
    Delivery mode
      - Group (including lecture, seminar, workshop)
      - Individualized (including tutorial, project,
      thesis)
    Traditional delivery media (face-to-face contact,
    print, audio)
    Technology-based delivery media
      - Interactive audio-video based
      - Computer based
  - Facilitating learning
  - Tutoring/mentoring
  - Advising/providing consumer information
  - Assessing
    Developing assessment mechanisms
  - Credentialing

- Research
- Public service
- Student support
- Academic support
- Institutional support
- Operation and maintenance of physical plant
- Auxiliary enterprises

Geographic (where functions are carried out)

- On campus
- Off campus
  - In-state
  - Out-of-state (by state)

Provider Resources

- Financial
  - Prices (charges to students)
  - Revenues and sources
  - Expenditures and objects
  - Expenditures for technology
      Infrastructure (for example, bandwidth)
      Equipment (for example, computers, routers,
          system software)
      Student faculty support (for example, training,
          help desk)
      Content (for example, courseware)
- Human resources
  - Types of human resources
      Faculty
      Facilitators
      Product developers
      Technicians
  - Characteristics of human resources
      Demographic descriptors
      Educational history
      Employment history with provider
      Conditions of employment
      Assignment/utilization activity

Outputs

Separation

- Technologies (see delivery media above)
- Licenses
  - Owned (for example, patents)
  - Purchased
- Facilities

Partners

Outcomes

Classification Structure Describing Learners

Characteristics

- Demographic
- Learner activity (current and prior)
  - K–12
  - Postsecondary
  - Employment
  - Civic
- Learner capabilities
- Goals
  - Educational success
  - Economic success
  - Success in transitions
  - Quality of life

Participation Patterns

- Interaction with providers
  - Identification of providers
  - Acquiring information
  - Receiving student services
  - Receiving advisement
  - Receiving tutoring, mentoring

- Being evaluated
- Receiving credentials
- Modes of student participation
  - Delivery modes
  - Delivery media
- Time frames/periodicity
  - Synchronous (years, terms, credit hours, clock hours)
  - Asynchronous (modules completed, time span of
      learning experience)
- Barriers to participation

Geographic (where learning takes place)

Financial

- Charges
- Financial aid
- Source of financial resources (for example, personal,
    governmental, employer)

Learner Resources

- Economic
- Access to technologies

Outcomes

- Basic skills
- Disciplinary knowledge
- Disciplinary breadth/concepts
- Occupation-specific skills
- Living and workplace skills
- Success rates
  - Synchronous
      Retention, success in subsequent learning experiences
  - Asynchronous
      Persistence toward learning goals

References

Green, K C. *Campus Computing, 1998: The National Study of Information Technology in American Higher Education*. Encino, Calif.: The Campus Computing Project, 1998.

National Center for Education Statistics. *Distance Education in Higher Education Institutions*. NCES 97-062. Washington, D.C.: National Center for Education Statistics, 1997. (See www.nces.ed.gov/NHES for information about the National Household Education Survey, of which the Adult Learner Survey is a component.)

National Center for Education Statistics. *1999 National Study of Postsecondary Faculty—Field Test Questionnaire*. Washington, D.C.: National Center for Education Statistics, 1999.

National Postsecondary Education Cooperative (NPEC). *Technology and Its Ramifications for Data Systems: Report of the Policy Panel on Technology*. NCES 98-279. Washington, D.C.: National Postsecondary Education Cooperative, 1998.

National Postsecondary Education Cooperative (NPEC). "Ramifications of Technology for Current Surveys, Recommendations of the Working Group." [nces.ed.gov/npec/projects.html]. June 1999.

Russell, A. B. *Advances in Statewide Higher Education Data Systems*. Denver: State Higher Education Executive Officers, 1995.

Terenzini, P. *Student Outcomes Information for Policy-Making*. Report prepared for the National Postsecondary Education Cooperative Working Group on Student Outcomes from a Policy Perspective. Washington, D.C.: National Postsecondary Education Cooperative, 1997.

Wolf, D. B., and Johnstone, S. M. "Cleaning Up the Language." *Change*, Jul.–Aug. 1999.

4

Technical Building Blocks to Enable E-Business

David L. Wasley

Access to on-line information resources and the use of electronic transactions increasingly augment the operation of modern colleges and universities. These resources and functions are important both internally and in collaboration with external partners. To reap the full benefits that these resources and processes can offer, all members of the campus community must be able to function easily and securely throughout this rapidly growing electronic information environment. Although campuses have made great strides toward developing robust and ubiquitous communications network infrastructures, the rich information environment envisioned in *Sustaining Excellence in the 21st Century* (Katz and West, 1992) will not be realized unless equally robust and ubiquitous enabling services are developed within the infrastructure of our campuses and throughout the higher education community.

I define the electronic information environment as that set of electronic information services, on-line resources, communications services, applications software, and workstations that enable us to teach and learn and work more effectively and without the

M. Stuart Lynn, a colleague and friend to most of us in the information technology community, provided ideas, advice, counsel, and encouragement in the creation of this chapter.

constraints of time or place. Within this environment, we need directories and other finding aids, credentials that can establish identity and roles for both consumer and supplier, and a myriad of other supporting services.

Infrastructure support services will enable easy and secure access to information resources, support authorized and verifiable transactions over the network, and make possible appropriate management of licensed materials and other intellectual property. With a coordinated approach, we will be able to leverage investments being made already in new applications on our campuses as well as across the higher education community.

As the electronic information environment grows and expands, it becomes necessary to acknowledge and implement certain constraints on users of these resources—the "network citizens" who navigate that environment. We must develop analogues of the administrative controls with which we are familiar in the traditional environment. These controls should be supported by generalized infrastructure services put in place and managed by the institution.

Existing access control and authentication mechanisms are largely a legacy of older centralized technology. Traditional institutional applications have been developed from the ground up, providing for all aspects of the process in an idiosyncratic way. Today we understand that many of the components of these applications have a great deal of commonality. These include a secure and reliable way to affirm that users of our resources are who they purport to be and that they are authorized to use the resources to which they seek access. There must be a source of definitive information regarding their affiliation with the campus as well as other business-related data. There must be directory services to help them find the resources they need. There must be standards and supporting services for encryption to secure data transmission and to create the digital equivalent of a personal signature. There must be efficient mechanisms to support accounting for the use of a wide variety of network-based resources as well as services that can be supported by network communications.

Lack of common general solutions for authentication, authorization, directory services, and encryption will impede the development of a broad range of information resources, from client-server financial systems to digital libraries. If properly designed, these technical building blocks can be combined and extended to form a set of common services, or "middleware," that will enable a wide variety of complex capabilities that are available almost transparently to the end user (see Figure 4.1). These new and critical middleware services will enable members of the academic community to become true universal network citizens and roam freely and securely, without undue let or hindrance, throughout the emerging electronic information environment.

The availability and use of these and other building blocks also can form the basis for more robust and efficient management of institutional resources. Rule-based authorization processes can support distributed operation and responsibility. Well-designed and reliable support services can help the campus protect intellectual property

Figure 4.1. Existing Applications with Independent Solutions to the Same Set of Problems

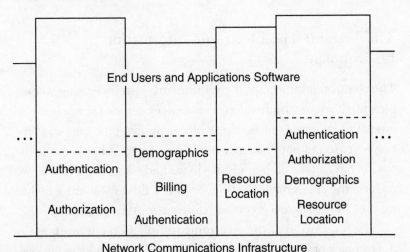

as well as institutional data. Data encryption standards and services will enable the reliable use of e-commerce within the institution and with external partners.

Differences among campuses in their information environment middleware services tend to inhibit sharing of resources, a tendency that will become exacerbated as critical new shared resources such as virtual digital libraries begin to emerge. Currently a faculty member or student at one campus who is visiting another campus must make special arrangements in order to make use of many of the services at the second campus. If the services require access control, the individual must acquire yet another password and account name. Coordinated middleware services can allow the identity and affiliations of any member of the higher education community to serve them wherever they may be working at the moment.

I will continue to use the metaphor of a network citizen traveling throughout the electronic information environment to illustrate the basic middleware building blocks. It is with the goal of catalyzing the development and implementation of the best technologies to implement these services within the higher education community that we begin this management tour of the electronic information environment.

The Terrain: The Electronic Information Environment

The electronic information environment is an increasingly complex territory in which valuable resources can be found, but it is foreign to our usual senses. Many of the familiar problems and processes are found here but take a different form. What is our identity? What can we do here? How do we find resources? How do we traverse the environment with safety? How do we account for what we use? Do we share a common reference for time or place?

The foundation of the electronic information environment is the complex of interconnected networks (including our campus networks) known as the global Internet. Accessible from desktops both within our campuses and via the Internet are an ever growing variety of databases, information servers, vendors doing business via e-commerce, computational servers, and a panoply of applications programs from e-mail to collaborative systems based on interactive virtual reality. E-commerce is developing rapidly in many forms and will enable reliable transaction of institutional business as well as new opportunities for individuals.

Our helpers in traveling the information environment are client software and programs that interact with other electronic entities by means of well-defined protocols. Just as in the analogue world, these protocols provide for successful interoperation among widely differing entities. The World Wide Web is an excellent example of this concept: the same set of complex text, graphics, audio, and video can be found and viewed on almost any modern computer regardless of what kind of computer might hold them. One significant advantage of this layered approach to complex systems is that individual pieces of the environment can be built or replaced without affecting the rest of the infrastructure. Another advantage is that end-user platforms can be tailored to different user communities and application needs. This layered approach must guide us in the development of essential information environment support services.

Passports: The Authentication Service

The fundamental support service that will empower the network citizen is a universal, distributed, reliable, and robust digital credential system. Just as travelers must carry their passport when entering a different country, network citizens should carry a recognized credential when entering the electronic information environment. This credential, which can be validated by any service encountered, will ensure the authentic identity of the individual holding it.

Passports are recognized as authoritative around the world because the issuing authority is recognized by international treaty. So too should the network credential be recognized as authoritative so that network citizens can visit various sites and resources without having to resort to site-specific identification. Instead of an international treaty, there must be agreements among cooperating administrative domains to trust each other's credentials. Such agreements are based on understanding the methodology and management of the process for issuing the credentials.

The concept of a digital credential that refers to a single electronic identity is powerful because it can enable easy access to resources for the traveler. The credential itself may not carry much information about the individual, much as the traditional passport carries not much more than a picture, an address, and a passport number. However, that passport number can be the key to determining additional attributes about the holder. In an analogous way, the digital credential should have an identifier (e-ID) that is unique to the credential holder and can be used as a key to discovering further identity information.

Relying on a single credential is fraught with the potential for abuse if it is mishandled. Since e-IDs will let travelers into many places, they must be issued only with strong assurance that individuals are who they claim to be. Once the e-ID is issued, the holder must recognize that it is an extension of his or her personal identity, protect it carefully, and never lend it to another person.

Even with reliable credentials, it will be desirable in many cases for an individual to have several e-IDs to be used for different purposes. All individuals and their organizations must consider the potential impact of a compromise of the security of any e-ID. For example, the manager of an administrative computing system might have an e-ID that carries with it special privileges. That e-ID should be used sparingly and only in conjunction with that system so that compromise of the more powerful e-ID would have consequences of a more limited scope and could be dealt with more readily. The system manager would use a less powerful e-ID when doing routine work, such as checking e-mail or writing reports.

An e-ID represents an assertion on the part of a registration authority that a known individual or entity is represented by that e-ID. If the registration authority is well designed and reliable, then services in cooperating administrative domains, or realms, can be comfortable accepting those externally registered e-IDs. Thus, in the general case, the e-ID must indicate not only the individual but also the registration authority that issued the e-ID. Ultimately this concept could be extended to commercial registration authorities so that, for example, high school students registered with a local electronic notary might be able to use their own credential's e-IDs in submitting electronic applications for admission to a college or university.

Once a campus has a robust digital credential issuance and authentication service in place with reliable operational support, all of the important campus server applications should be adapted to use this system. Parts of this process could take a long time since many applications are vendor supported and vendors are not yet responding to this broader vision. Until there is a well-established generalized authentication service, each server or application has little choice but to implement its own idiosyncratic method of authentication, and the network citizen must deal individually with each one encountered.

Tickets and Passes: Attribute and Eligibility Databases

Eligibility, as distinct from authentication (which warrants the identity of a particular user), is an equally important support service in the electronic information environment. Eligibility helps define what network citizens may do or that to which they may gain access. It may be based on a person's e-ID or on any set of attributes associated with that e-ID, such as the person's affiliation with or within the institution, role, or current status. Often it is desirable to separate authentication service from eligibility and attribute functions, and it may be desirable to support them on different servers.

Eligibility does not necessarily imply authorization. The network citizen may be eligible to gain access to a resource, but at the time access is requested, the service might be oversubscribed or otherwise unavailable. For example, holding an airplane ticket may not result in authorization to board that flight. Authorization is a function of the service or application based on specific business rules. These rules might take into account a variety of factors in addition to the individual's identity, such as time of day, location of the individual, or the availability of resources.

In the historical model of mainframe computing, authentication (often referred to as access control) and authorization were often closely linked. Authorization usually was determined by loose association of attributes with the user account identifier (for example, "root" or "user, group, and other" in Unix systems) or by tables of authorized users. Since each system kept its own set of authorization data, management of these data in a consistent way across a large number of servers and client platforms was problematic, although a number of projects attempted to address aspects of this dilemma. Little thought was given to generalized information environment management mechanisms until the number of different systems and services began to grow dramatically.

Today we need generalized and scalable network-based mechanisms not only for authentication but also for eligibility and attribute information. As an example of how this might be provided, suppose the network citizen requests access to a restricted database. The database server can simply query a specified attribute server, supplying the network citizen's e-ID, and receive information on the roles, affiliations, or other attributes defined for that individual. The database server then can apply a prescribed set of business rules to determine whether that particular network citizen is to be allowed access to the restricted data.

Suppose the network citizen's affiliation with the institution is "full professor and dean of the college." This might imply eligibility to view college budgetary data and approve spending plans and personnel actions, as well as to gain access to academic records and information. The same person might also be appointed to a multi-campus task force on student diversity and because of that affiliation be eligible to retrieve sensitive student ethnicity and gender data. A database server that returned roles and affiliations for any given institutional e-ID would make management of this type of generalized eligibility much easier.

Such eligibility or affiliation data might be useful in transactions external to the institution as well. Appropriate individuals in any department could be given authority to submit electronic data interchange (EDI) purchase orders over the network, for example. A different set of individuals could have authority to approve payment of EDI-based invoices electronically. Workflow systems could identify individuals who need to be informed of such transactions for possible post-transaction audit.

Whereas administration of an attribute service should be hierarchical and coordinated centrally, responsibility for actual eligibility data with respect to any given service should be distributed to conform with campus management structure. This is primarily an administrative rather than a technical issue. Suffice it to say that developing and managing a database service that combines all important attributes, roles, and affiliations and allows them to be managed by the office of record would provide important generality while maintaining the institution's established administrative structure.

Who's There? The Demographics Database Service

One particularly vexing problem is the maintenance of accurate personal data, such as home address, campus office address, or preferred e-mail address. Today there are far too many different databases wherein the same data are entered, usually by different individuals, from separate forms that must be filled out repetitively by the person who actually "owns" the information. For example, in many cases the same individual is both a student and an employee, which means that the same personal data often are maintained by entirely separate offices. Clearly it would be desirable to have a single comprehensive database of record that would hold information about all members of the campus community and in which personal data could be maintained by the relevant individual or appropriately designated staff.

With strong authentication and a well-designed attribute service, it would be possible to build such a demographics database system. It might well be combined with a basic eligibility service so that a single database system supports both. Fields within a record would have associated rules for access or updating. All institutional applications that require use of personal data would use this comprehensive demographics database by either periodic downloading or indirect relational reference. In particular, on-line directory services for locating campus community members would use this authoritative database as their data source.

Campus network citizens could be responsible for maintaining all of their own personal data and also could check on the completeness or accuracy of other attribute data, such as payroll title or salary, status toward a degree, or the parameters of their employee benefits.

Maps and Guidebooks: Directory Services

Information services and resources abound on campuses and beyond. The community of users changes and moves about, and the topology of the network changes periodically. How does a network citizen find anyone else or any particular service or information?

The Domain Name Service was the first widespread directory service in support of the information environment. Other common directories exist today, such as directories of people and searchable databases of information resources. Many more kinds of maps and guidebooks are needed to serve the new and complex information resources we are deploying. For example, the network citizen might want to find an on-line copy of Van Gogh's *Child with Orange* and the nearest color printer that she or he is eligible to use and that is capable of high-resolution, large-format printing. New resource location services must support more complex data and search strategies.

A well-managed set of directory servers and search engines for information objects will help the network citizen discover resources and navigate easily throughout the electronic information environment.

Safe Passage: Encryption and Digital Signatures

Authentication and access control alone are not sufficient to guarantee safe passage throughout the electronic information environment. Passwords can be guessed or stolen, data can be monitored in transit, and identities sometimes can be forged. The strongest defense against these challenges involves the use of modern encryption methods to ensure privacy of data transmission and create the digital equivalent of a pen-and-ink signature.

Our networks are truly open systems, which is one of their strengths as well as a source of many vulnerabilities. Any transmission might be intercepted, and any data received might be questionable. Attacking computers on the Internet has become a rampant obsession among certain curious and occasionally antisocial groups. Fortunately, modern encryption technology offers potential solutions for most of these concerns.

Encryption of data while in transit can protect privacy as well as the confidentiality and integrity of data. The technology required to implement data encryption has become commonplace and should be considered for all administrative or other institutional business applications. Encryption alone may not guarantee authenticity, however. We need the equivalent of a seal or at least a recognized signature associated with the contents of the document.

A digital signature must be some set of data that cannot be forged and that binds the contents of a digital document to a specific individual, role, or other entity. It must be something that only the signing entity could have created and must be verifiable by anyone in the electronic information environment.

Standards now exist for creating this type of digital signature using public key cryptography (PKC). Clearly digital signatures of this sort would enable a wide variety of institutional business to be transacted over the network with at least as reliable verification and auditability as we have now with paper forms and manual signatures.

A public key infrastructure (PKI) is critical to enabling the use of encryption and digital signatures. Fundamental to the PKI is a unique pair of very large prime numbers, generated for each credential holder, that are keys used for encryption and decryption of information. Software on the network citizen's workstation generates this pair of encryption keys and gives one of them (the "public" key) to the PKI certificate authority (CA). The other key (the "private" key) is closely guarded by the network citizen. The CA stores the public key in a directory along with the PKI certificate. Upon request, the CA or directory server provides any registered user's public key to any application that needs it.

In addition to support of the local community, a CA must have a way to find other trusted CAs on other campuses or anywhere else in the electronic information environment. This ability is part of an overall PKI and may be implemented in a number of different ways.

The basis for trusting a traditional signature is either direct knowledge or the ability to look it up in an archive maintained by a trusted authority, such as a bank. In the digital world, trust must be established through preestablished contracts based on mutual understanding of business practices, the basis for registering individuals with the CA, and the viability of the cooperating CAs.

The resulting so-called web of trust must be scalable to millions of users in thousands of locations. This can be achieved through a hierarchical model wherein a community-based CA registers subordinate CAs after verifying their viability. A consortium of college and university campuses, for example, could operate such a certificate authority and the associated services on behalf of its members. This CA in turn could register under national and international CAs to allow fully general and trustworthy access to verifiable public key directory servers anywhere in the world. A campus PKI with its root certificate authority also could register subordinate CAs for departments, the library, or special-purpose requirements.

Until and unless encryption mechanisms and support services are in use, no one should send anything of value or of a sensitive nature, such as a credit card number, over the data network.

Sharing Limited Resources: License Servers

The network citizen is now equipped with the basic tools for verifying identity, invoking authority, and concluding transactions safely. These capabilities enable easy and appropriate access to a wide variety of resources within our electronic information environment. Unfortunately, not all of those resources are without significant cost to the institution.

A traditional library might hold five copies of a popular book or journal. Ideally this would be enough to meet the peak demand at any one time for this resource. It would not be economical to purchase one copy for every registered patron, yet we often provide software and other resources in this cost-inefficient way.

It is quite possible for software or other digital resources to be purchased by subscription, much like printed documents today. The cost of such a subscription would be based at least in part on the size of the simultaneous user community. For example, a physics department might purchase a subscription for twenty simultaneous "users" of a virtual physics laboratory software package. During laboratory classes, the students make use of the software on computers located in the facility. In the evening, when doing homework, up to twenty students could make use of the same "subscription" to run the software on their own personal computer.

One way to enable this type of sharing of expensive resources is a network-based license server (NLS). The NLS serves as a clearinghouse to ensure conformance with the terms of the institution's subscription. An early implementation of the NLS concept was available with the Apollo domain computers. Macintosh and PC versions of license servers offer similar capabilities. Standardizing on an openly available NLS technology would enable publishers to develop products that could fit readily into our electronic information environment. A single NLS could moderate access to a wide variety of licensed resources, including databases and documents as well as software.

Paying the Bills: Automated Debit and Unified Invoicing

Much of the electronic information environment today is accessible without direct cost to the network citizen. However, as the real costs become significant, the campus may need to find efficient ways at least to account for the usage of expensive resources and possibly allocate some of the acquisition and support costs toward the end users. A building block that could help achieve this is an efficient network accounting server.

Ultimately every member of the campus community, as defined in the campus's demographics database and corresponding eligibility servers, could have one or more "virtual accounts." Transactions for services would be posted to a designated network accounting server using encrypted data flows. A wide variety of network citizen services, from print-on-demand syllabi to lunches and storehouse items, could be accounted for in this way.

The network citizen should expect a single statement each month describing all services used and any costs incurred anywhere within the institution. This might include transactions with external partners as well. Eventually this monthly accounting could result in an automated debit against an external financial service, much like debit cards are used today.

What Time Is It? The Network Time Server

It may not seem obvious but many of the services we are developing need to have a common frame of reference for time. Billing information, for example, must show accurately the date and approximate time of the transaction. Network management information often needs time stamps to be accurate to within a few milliseconds. Electronic postmark or notary services must have an auditable date and time guaranteed to be within a known degree of accuracy. Thus, an important element in the set of enabling services within our information environment is the network time server.

Technologies in support of network time services exist today and are deployed on most campuses. However, not all of these are synchronized with each other or with a universal time standard, such as the National Institute of Standards and Technology broadcast standard time service.

Even where synchronized network time servers exist, not all essential end systems can take advantage of them yet. Campus information technology managers must understand the importance of this element of distributed systems and take appropriate steps to ensure integration of this service.

Our network citizens may wish to set their own "electronic watch" from this service as well. Most modern workstations can be configured with automatic utilities to accomplish this.

Where to Now?

The building blocks I have identified are all part of a larger set of standards that comprise an information technology architecture. The basic enabling services include the following features:

- A coordinated set of authentication servers

- An attribute and demographic database server on each campus that can include a wide variety of information, including affiliation and eligibility data

- Directory and resource location servers

- PKI servers that manage certificates and public encryption keys for individual users and make possible digital signature verification

- Electronic license servers in support of site-licensed software, library materials, and databases

- Billing transaction servers that can handle a large volume of small-value debit records extremely efficiently

- Time servers and digital notary servers that form the basis for reliable and verifiable on-line content and digital institutional archives

Figure 4.2 shows how the building blocks might relate to each other and to the communications system and applications programs. Other building blocks might include software version control servers

Figure 4.2. Information Environment Building Blocks with Common Interoperable Solutions for Basic Supporting Services

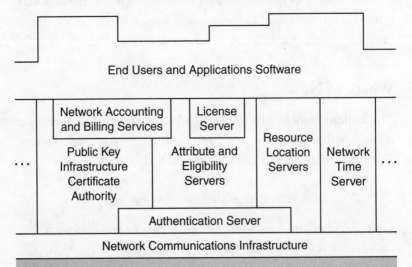

to ensure that campus users have access to the latest version of critical application programs, and alias servers to support consistent mapping between e-IDs and e-mail addresses or traditional identifiers such as employee number or student ID number. Current and potential technologies behind each of the building blocks described above are in different states of development and deployment.

With persistent vision and cooperative efforts, we can refine and deploy appropriate versions of all these enabling services over the next few years. If we do not start now, it may become very difficult to develop and retrofit a coordinated set of these services later. There is much to be done before network citizens are fully empowered.

Reference

Katz, R. N., and West, R. P. *Sustaining Excellence in the 21st Century: A Vision and Strategies for College and University Administration*. Boulder, Colo.: CAUSE, 1992. [www.educause.edu/ir/library/pdf/PUB3008.pdf].

5

Information Policy to Support Campus E-Business

Richard N. Katz

The unprecedented flow of information across networks and between organizations, coupled with the power of computers to extract, compile, organize, and republish information, has made e-business possible. These same capabilities are also raising significant concerns and issues related to the appropriate use of institutional information and the protection of information originating or residing in college and university information systems.

The closing chapter of this book describes the developmental phase facing colleges and universities today on the road to enabling e-business as one of integration. Our progress in adopting e-business in higher education will be enabled or constrained by institutions' abilities to develop, implement, enforce, and automate complex rules that authorize these consumers to partake of university services—for example:

- What rights will distant learners have regarding access to licensed university information resources?
- How can colleges and universities protect usage logs that record student and faculty library consumption activity for materials licensed from third parties?

I thank Gary Gatien of the University of Michigan for his significant research in support of this chapter.

- What information can and should development offices acquire and maintain on prospective donors?

The privacy, access, ownership, and security issues posed by e-business are extraordinarily complex and represent as much a set of cultural, behavioral, and policy issues as technical ones.

Colleges and universities have long—and correctly—been described as self-governing anarchies or adhocracies. Higher education's hallowed and well-established traditions of self-governance and shared governance are responsible for our remarkable history of achievement, service, and innovation. These traditions also make integration hard. In many ways, achieving the necessary level of technical integration to enable e-business is the least complex aspect of preparing the institution for e-business. Many campus chief information officers (CIOs) understand what it means to reorient systems from their current functional office views to the end-user views (student, parent, alumni, inter-enterprise) that e-business will demand. In most cases, the technical tools to achieve this kind of integration exist. In short, technical integration is a significant issue that can be addressed by vision, talent, and money. The thornier integration challenges are cultural and relate to role definitions, authority and power, and values. These issues will define the boundaries of an institution's approach to, and its likelihood of success in, implementing e-business.

The Need for a Policy Framework to Support E-Business

In a farsighted article, Graves, Jenkins, and Parker (1995) at the University of North Carolina described the development of an electronic information policy framework. As e-business drives the Internet and Web from an infrastructure for storing static information to one over which much of the institutional mission is delivered, the need for such a policy framework becomes overwhelming. Although sound information policies will not guarantee entry into the world of e-business, lack of these policies will bar the door. Colleges and universities will need to develop a cohesive and consistent set of policies to guide the members of their community in a number of areas, including the following:

- Digital identity and the access to institutional technology and information resources

- Use of the institution's name and trademarks

- Acquisition, retention, and disposition of information resources

- Ownership of information in institutional systems and the management of intellectual property rights

Each of these issues is enormously complex, and colleges and universities worldwide have struggled with them for years. No attempt will be made in this chapter to specify solutions in these areas. Rather, the purpose of this chapter is to relate the necessity of developing a holistic electronic information policy framework to efforts to implement e-business.

Digital Identity and Access to Institutional Technology and Information Resources

Chapter Four of this book introduces in considerable detail the issue of digital identity. In the technical context, colleges and universities must develop the means to authenticate an individual as himself or herself, recognize the individual as a member of the institutional community, and confer on or deny this individual different rights and authorities as a community citizen. In physical reality, these activities are transacted in a variety of complex formal or informal ways. We can demand photo ID cards, check signature files, or wave to the familiar librarian who regulates access to the closed stacks.

The regulation of access to institutional resources in the physical context is governed by a tapestry of policies, procedures, customs, norms, and historical happenstance that computers are not yet intelligent enough to deal with. Instead, computers depend on precise information that derives absolute answers to the following questions: (1) are you who you claim to be, and (2) are you allowed to . . . [consume this service, enter this building, use this parking lot]?

Not only is this a technical challenge of enormous proportions, it is a policy quagmire that requires colleges and universities to make explicit and public distinctions about the rights and privileges that accrue to different members of the academy. What rights does the president's spouse really have? What rights do lecturers have, relative to career-ladder faculty? These policy issues will become more complex as colleges and universities move into distance education and implement cradle-to-grave strategies to create relationships with promising applicants, lifelong learners, and potential donors.

Of course, it is important to note that for public institutions, managing access to institutional information must be situated in the context of public records laws, which themselves are hard to reduce to simple rules that can be automated.

Use of the Institution's Name and Trademarks

The Internet and the World Wide Web are, among other things, a publishing infrastructure. Web browser technology is relatively simple to program as well as to use, allowing "a thousand flowers to bloom." At nearly every college and university, a myriad of operational and dead Web pages make volumes of campus information and misinformation available to anyone with an Internet connection.

Many institutions provide incoming students with sufficient disk storage to encourage their development of personal Web sites. Of course, into every flower garden will come the occasional weed, snail, or other predator. From a policy perspective, the challenge posed by the Internet and the Web is the challenge of cultural integration. Colleges and universities must specify policies that regulate the appropriate use of these very public resources. At stake in this extraordinarily complex area to govern are a variety of serious legal and public relations issues, including these:

- Pornographic materials on official institutional sites

- Sale of advertising on pages containing campus trademarks

- Creation of fraudulent sites

- Commercial use of campus resources for personal gain

- Trademark infringement

- Neglect of sites that make inaccurate, anachronistic, and obsolete information available to legislators, trustees, donors, auditors, and others

All of these issues can and will emerge within the broader policy contexts that typically respect and encourage free expression by members of the institution's community. As Graves, Jenkins, and Parker (1995) advise, "Any policy will need to balance the institution's role in protecting access to sensitive or potentially objectionable information and its role in supporting an individual's right of free expression" (p. 18). This difficult balancing act is hardly new, but is complicated by the levels of integration anticipated by e-business applications.

Acquisition, Retention, and Disposition of Information Resources

E-business, in much of the popular literature, begins with something called "e-tailing": the marketing of the enterprise to its existing or prospective clients. In one context, higher education institutions have been doing this for years. Each year, colleges and universities acquire the files of high school students who achieve high scores on the PSAT and shower these college-bound tenth and eleventh graders with literature extolling the virtues of their campus. In an e-business context, smart and aggressive institutions will acquire more and more information in the competition for the "best" students. These institutions will likely develop robust profiles of students to match against the target profiles of successful applicants. Similarly, the pathologies of university hospital patients will be profiled for matching against promising experimental drugs and therapies for possible targeting of such patients for clinical trials.

These practices are entrepreneurial, effective (relative to their goals), and probably beneficial; certainly college-bound students want to be discovered and patients want access to the best modes of treatment available. However, the unprecedented ability of institutions to acquire personal information, combine this information in unique ways, and store massive amounts of this information on individuals who may, or may not, be part of the institutional community will raise significant privacy and security issues. New policies regarding what kind of information is to be collected, how this information is to be used, and how long it is to be retained will become increasingly important. The failure to develop new standards of practice in this area will invite new regulation of this area of institutional activity. The issue of individual and institutional access to this kind of information will also rise in importance and must be dealt with explicitly in campus information policy.

In addition to developing the technologies and policies to ensure privacy and secure and protect information under institutional management, colleges and universities will need to devise and implement new policies to describe, manage, and protect related classes of information. Such classes of information include confidential information (tenure and promotion files), proprietary information (patents, trademarks, copyrights), privileged information (attorney-client communications, counseling files), and trade information (public and private research activities). E-business, among other things, assumes an unprecedented level of interoperation among the systems and data resources of "trading partners." In the future, campus suppliers will have access to institutional procurement systems, as will publishers, high schools, consortium partners, and others. This integration of systems and information will demand that policies and contracts regulate the acquisition, use, retention, and disposition by others in the newly extending community. This has already become a complex area of policy development at research universities, where the university values of open sharing of research findings clash with desires of private clinical research sponsors to protect information as proprietary.

A final area of concern under this broad umbrella is the management of licensed software and information resources. Campus information policy must respect the rights of authors and distributors. Evolving technologies and law will likely enhance authors' and distributors' ability to track the use of their licensed property and perhaps even to implement campuswide penalties when infringements are identified.

Ownership of Information and Intellectual Property Rights

Information policy must seek to distinguish the ownership status of information embodied in institutionally owned digital storage and transport media from the responsibilities for managing this information. Information policies should strive to define the standards and care with which information resources must be managed, while recognizing the inherently decentralizing tendencies of networked information and resources. Most information policy frameworks that address networked information define and articulate a concept of information stewardship that allows the web of campus-related information to evolve in a fashion that balances the needs of individuals and local campus units with those of the institution as a whole.

Perhaps the most complex aspect of preparing the campus information policy environment for e-business is the set of policy issues surrounding the ownership and management of intellectual property generated on the campus. Colleges and universities have developed robust policies for the ownership and management of intellectual property protected by patents, but the rights to intellectual property developed by faculty and protected by copyright have traditionally remained with individual faculty. In fact, the total economic value of published college and university intellectual property has been small historically, and the institutional investment in the creation of this property has also been small.

The application of Internet, Web, and other information technologies to the core educational mission of higher education is changing all of this. Today, pioneering faculty are investing considerable time and energy to Web-enable their courses. Institutions in many cases are partnering with these faculty by providing grants to purchase release time from other obligations and by placing a variety of technical tools at the faculty's disposal. For the first time, faculty course materials organized in this fashion can reach beyond the confines of the classroom, hence changing simultaneously the cost structure, the investment model, and the economic value of traditional course materials. Courses created in this fashion become courseware and begin to accrue many of the attributes of books, which also are evolving to become more interactive.

As the e-learning aspect of the e-business revolution evolves, institutions, their faculty, and publishers are looking at course materials as scalable economic goods that can be modularized. New pedagogical standards are evolving in concert with new neuroscientific findings about the learning process. Institutions such as the University of Phoenix and Great Britain's Open University are investing millions of dollars in curricula for networked delivery. Faculty course notes on the Web are being reportedly pirated and repackaged for distribution by new proprietary e-business enterprises. Clearly the new potentials posed by the integrated technologies of e-business suggest the need for new policies regarding the ownership and management of rights to faculty course materials.

Framed creatively, this discussion and faculty and institutional investments can draw new students into the campus community and in some cases bring new revenue to the institution. Such changes are, however, countercultural and could also lead to new divisions on the campus. As noted in Chapter Six, e-business is likely to change the way institutions operate. It is a mission-critical undertaking that will challenge longstanding institutional policies and will therefore demand the careful application of change management techniques and processes.

Elements of an Integrated Policy Framework

Although each institution will develop a policy that best reflects its priorities, strategies, values, and history, a framework should contain some common elements. The list that follows is offered as a starting point.

Critical Assumptions

The institution will balance the rights of individuals with the institution's responsibility to make information available to support the mission. The role of the central campus is to articulate the standards of data access and integrity and to differentiate user rights and privileges so as to achieve such balance. The following key assumption will need to be articulated:

- Under what conditions (responsibilities of resource users) and for what members of the community are access to the network, network-based services, and networked information a basic right of the campus community?

Operating Principles

Policies are by definition value laden. Institutions can be well served by considering bounding the framework by principles. At the University of North Carolina (UNC), information policy is bounded by principles that do the following:

- Identify the responsibility for making information available

- Limit the institution's regulatory responsibility for information for which it is not responsible

- Assume institutional responsibility for defining access privileges to its information for classes of users

The UNC policy framework and those of other leading institutions also outline in broad terms legal, ethical, technical, governance, and economic issues for the purpose of acculturating the policy reader to the complexity of the issues and the basic values of the institution.

Information Access and Security

It will be important to establish the notion that institutional electronic information resources—including data, applications, systems,

*"We don't want just anyone coming in here and making toast.
Type in your password."*

Source: Copyright © 1998 by Sidney Harris.

hardware, software, and networks—are valuable. Institutional assets, including electronic information resources, must be protected according to the nature of the risk and to the sensitivity and criticality of the resource being protected. Information policy should endeavor to identify major classes of information assets requiring protection and assigning to them differential levels of protection. Information classes might include privileged information, personal information, personnel information, and public records.

Areas in which security-related policies need to be addressed include the following, paraphrased from the University of California's "Business and Finance Bulletin IS-3: Electronic Information Security" (1998):

- *Logical security.* The policy should identify security measures to be enforced through software, network, or procedural controls (version management, and so forth), as well as communications security and reduction of risk from intrusive computer software. Various measures include end-user access controls, system administration access controls, applications software development and change control, and controls on data backup, retention, data privacy, and data transfers and downloads. Encryption policies will also need to be developed as these capabilities become ubiquitous, as will policies that specify which applications and resources must be protected by firewalls.

- *Physical security.* Even in an e-business environment, there are physical disaster controls and access controls (for example, check stock and other financial instruments) that must be covered by institutional policy.

- *Managerial security.* Although there are unique risks inherent in the management of electronic and particularly networked information resources, many of the

risks remain people related. An information policy
framework should attempt to integrate institutional
policy related to bonding and background checking for
personnel with access to sensitive and critical information. Procedures to implement such policies should
also identify the processes for altering authorities when
changes in duties or employment status occur.

- *Responsibilities*. An information policy framework must
  identify both those responsible for maintaining the
  policy and those responsible for its implementation.
  Ideally, policy compliance escalation procedures should
  be specified.

- *Definitions and authorities*. A policy framework should
  define key terms such as *authorized user, disaster,*
  and *security*. Information management roles such as
  stewardship and proprietorship should also be defined.
  Regulations and laws that govern an institution's access
  and security policies should be referenced, including
  public records law.

- *Digital certificates*. An emerging technology to meet the
  needs of electronic security in the networked context is
  the use of public key infrastructure and digital certificates. This technology is being developed to address
  the authorization and authentication issue described
  at length in Chapter Four. Institutions that implement
  certificate authorities and digital certificates also will
  need to develop congruent policies that identify
  processes for approving authorities, standards for certificates, and identification of certificates. Policies
  will have to be enacted that govern whether certificates are issued to individuals, servers, or certificate
  authorities; what the responsibilities of these authori-

ties are; and what the expiry dates of these certificates will be. Finally, policy in this evolving arena will need to describe the processes for registering and issuing certificates, maintaining a repository of certificates and public keys, revoking or renewing certificates, and managing the certificate authority's private key.

Disaster Protection

The information policy framework should describe the institution's plans, policies, and procedures for ensuring business continuity, including plans for testing critical systems periodically.

The disaster recovery plan should identify emergency response procedures and specify teams of personnel responsible for responding to emergency situations.

E-Mail

Although e-mail is not specifically a tool of e-business, its governance as a critical element of the overall campus information policy framework is critical. Institutions are advised to develop specific policies related to e-mail that establish the following elements:

- E-mail accounts as institutional property

- The institution's service commitments regarding e-mail

- The ownership of information produced and received using institutional mail accounts

- Institutional access to information in mail accounts under normal or extraordinary (emergency, investigative, and so forth) conditions

- Allowable use, including use for individual commercial gain, representations, and false identity

- Security and confidentiality of information in institutional mail accounts

- Individual and institutional responsibilities and authorities for ensuring compliance with policy

Intellectual Property

Policy related to the management and ownership of intellectual property is highly complex. For intellectual property not developed on campus and covered by copyrights, patents, licenses, or other contracts, the policy parameters tend to be straightforward:

- Software resident on institutional hardware must be used according to the terms specified under the appropriate software license agreement.

- The institution is responsible for compliance with licenses entered into by the institution on behalf of members of its community. It should maintain the right to revoke licensed privileges in cases where violations have been identified. Substantial violations of license conditions should be specified under policy, as should the process for investigating alleged misuse and for implementing remedial action.

- Information resources such as databases, books, and journal articles are governed by copyright law or by license agreements with their publisher. Institutional policy should affirm the rights of authors, publishers, and distributors to their intellectual property; define what constitutes fair use in the context of law and licenses; and identify the processes for investigating alleged misuse and for implementing remedial action.

For intellectual property developed on campus, the institution must distinguish between so-called works for hire and other works produced in the discharge of an employee's work-related roles:

- The ownership of a work for hire is generally assumed to be the property of the institution. The information policy framework should make explicit reference to the institution's assumptions about what works are considered to be works for hire and what ownership rights the institution wishes to assert. This policy should also specify what rights individuals who are creating works for hire may have (publication of a work report in a professional journal) and what the process is for securing individual access to such works.

- The ownership of other intellectual property produced by members of the campus community is more likely to fall under an institution's faculty handbook, or in policy covering patents, or even conflict of interest and commitment (Thompson, 1999). As the boundaries between course materials and published materials begin to blur, institutions will need to revisit the ownership issues as part of an integrated information policy framework.

Conclusion

Policy by its nature is soft, squishy, and difficult. Policy development and the policy environment are inherently value laden, and therefore there are no detailed instructions for policy formulation. Policies are for the most part context specific. A Bible college's definition of appropriate use of technology will likely differ from that of a public research university.

Policy can be integrative, and integration is the mandate that looms ahead for institutions seeking to implement e-business solutions. Colleges and universities anticipating the move to e-business must recall that e-business in many areas is not merely the application of new technology to old processes. E-business applications will open new vistas and create new risks. Extending the name and reach of your college and university can and will swell the ranks of members of your communities. As communities grow, opportunities grow. And along with opportunities come fraud, abuse, and misuse. An integrated information policy framework will be hard to institute. On the other hand, an integrated, e-business environment without a supporting policy framework will be nearly impossible to manage.

References

Graves, W., Jenkins, C., and Parker, A. "Development of an Electronic Information Policy Framework." *CAUSE/EFFECT*, Summer 1995, pp. 15–23. [www.educause.edu/ir/library/pdf/cem9524.pdf].

Thompson, D. "Intellectual Property Meets Information Technology." *Educom Review*, 1999, *34*, 14–21. [www.educause.edu/ir/library/html/erm99022.html].

University of California. "Business and Finance Bulletin IS-3: Electronic Information Security." [www.ucop.edu/ucophome/policies/bfb/is3.pdf]. Nov. 1998.

6

Preparing Your Campus for E-Business

Jillinda J. Kidwell, John Mattie, Michael Sousa

From the boardroom to the executive suite to the music department, campus administrators are beginning to engage in e-business initiatives, enticed by the lure of profitable new markets, greater student satisfaction, and potential cost savings. Vendors are capitalizing on the growing sense of urgency taking hold on campus to sell technology-enabled teaching tools, put courses on-line, and provide Web portals for students, faculty, and administrators. The pressure to "do something" increases each time a new joint venture is announced or a college receives a sales pitch from the exploding list of new vendors.

While it is tempting to simply sign one of the many contracts sitting on your desk, it is important to look first. Even for those who have taken the plunge and are pursuing one or more strategies for doing e-business, due diligence will provide real dividends. These initiatives are new ventures. Often there are no well-established courses to follow. Yet in spite of the novelty of your e-business strategy, you can take steps to manage the risks. Whether your e-business initiative is an electronic commerce application, Web-enabled student services, or distance education, your institution will benefit by thinking through the drivers, implications, framework for evolving your e-business strategy, strategies for the future, and lessons presented in this chapter.

E-Business Drivers in Higher Education

Will e-business applications become widespread in higher education? Although these applications are being used primarily among
early adopters, it is clear, when one examines the drivers, that
e-business will garner more than ephemeral attention. According
to some, the adoption of such applications in higher education will
become pervasive as students and prospective students look to these
applications for convenience and institutions seek to expand markets, lower costs, and provide improved customer service. Among
the drivers for higher education institutions to develop an e-business
strategy are these:

- The rising popularity of the Internet

- Increasingly demanding customers and unrelenting
  expectations for expedited services

- Continuing cost constraints

- Opportunities for new revenues

Rising Popularity of the Internet

The Internet is fast approaching ubiquitous access, especially among
college students, due to increasing computer ownership and commonplace Internet usage. Specifically, 55 percent of college students
own a computer, and over 92 percent have access to one. Furthermore, many of these computer users are active Internet users. Among
four-year college students, 85.4 percent use e-mail, and 86.6 percent
use the Internet.

Current obstacles are expected to dissipate in the future. The
biggest complaint today about the Internet—its slowness if connected
through a modem—will eventually disappear as bandwidth, particularly to "the last mile," becomes more abundant. The technologies that
will make this possible will be cable modems, asynchronous transfer

mode (ATM), xDSL, frame relay, low-earth-orbiting satellites, and an advanced Internet.

Increasing Demands and Expectations

Today's students are technologically savvy and proficient. They have grown up accustomed to automated teller machines, toll-free numbers, next-day delivery, and even the Internet. They are able to procure books, CDs, and even term papers (much to the chagrin of educators) over the World Wide Web and increasingly expect the same type of instant fulfillment of needs and wants. Queues on campus—for course registration, feedback from advisers, financial aid decisions, degree audits, and other services—will be met with disdain and vocal dissatisfaction.

Similarly, due to services that they are able to receive from other Web-based companies, students—and staff and faculty—increasingly will expect services to be available on a 24x7 basis (twenty-four hours a day, seven days a week) and to be personalized based on their needs and interests. As in other industries, only the Web and associated e-business applications can provide this functionality for colleges and universities. For example, Amazon.com remembers book preferences and provides suggestions to customers. Can on-line course registration applications provide suggestions on course electives based on past preferences or other variables such as meeting time, professor, learning style and assignments, academic area, number of credits, background of fellow students, prerequisites, impact on degree completion, instructor and course rating by previous students, preparedness for other classes, or even cost of textbooks? Can a Web-based application recall a principal investigator's area of interest and provide customized information and services accordingly?

Colleges and universities increasingly will need to understand the functionality resident in best-in-class portals (gateways to the Web) and service providers from other industries to anticipate student, faculty, and staff expectations. Researching the current services and plans available only at other colleges and universities will be insufficient and shortsighted.

Continuing Cost Constraints

Even with favorable demographics and unique economic prosperity (and record tax receipts), cost pressures continue on the campuses of colleges and universities. In the early 1990s, colleges faced deficits that mandated across-the-board cutbacks. Today, across-the-board cutbacks have been replaced by the need for rapid, strategic reallocations. Resources are needed for enterprise systems implementations, expanded use of technology in the classroom, investments in technological infrastructure, capital improvements, and other mission-critical expenditures. Budget processes throughout the industry are being redesigned to unearth resources from underperforming programs or inefficient processes to enable reinvestment in higher-priority initiatives.

The search to do more with less will continue unfettered, so that colleges and universities can aggressively pursue strategic opportunities in the midst of increasing competition. To accomplish these objectives, institutions increasingly will look to e-business applications to reduce administrative costs, especially in business-to-business services, by reducing manual activities.

Opportunities for New Revenues

Universities increasingly have diversified revenue streams with research grants and contracts (with an increasing percentage from the corporate sector), fundraising receipts, advertising, and continuing-education students. Each of these areas will require the utilization of e-business approaches to generate new—and even retain current—revenues. As has been documented, colleges and universities increasingly depend on continuing-education students, revenues, and "profits." However, distance education will become a required core competency for succeeding in continuing education.

Technology-based education—e-learning—is growing at a faster rate than classroom education, and leading to a dramatic shift. According to International Data Corporation, technology-based information technology (IT) training is forecast to increase to 55 percent of U.S. training by 2002, up from 21 percent in 1998, thereby displacing classroom training as the method of choice for delivering IT-related education and training (Moretti and Johnston, 1998). Admittedly, the IT industry is an early adopter of electronic education and training. However, as colleges and universities seek to increase—or even just retain—continuing-education revenues, their success will depend on their ability to make the transition to and integrate technology-based approaches.

Implications

The business case for adopting an e-business strategy is compelling, and the urgency to do so will grow. We have identified four immediate implications as to how this expected change in delivery of services will affect colleges and universities in the short term:

1. In all areas, multiple vendors with a broad array of products will cause increased confusion as institutions determine whether to build or buy and compete or collaborate.
2. The Internet will affect process, organization, and policies.
3. The Internet will raise a host of other new issues—tax, legal, security, and skills.
4. Integrating information management will be a crucial challenge to enable institutions to leverage fully the benefits of doing business electronically.

More Options, Increased Confusion

Historically, colleges and universities assumed responsibilities for all components of the value chain—the strategically relevant activities in which an organization engages, how these components interact, and how they contribute to competitive advantage (Porter, 1985). The influx of e-business vendors in higher education across a variety of processes will present choices and complexity. Where do core competencies exist? Should an institution build or buy? Should an institution compete or collaborate? Table 6.1 illustrates a sample of process areas and new entrants that are providing e-business applications and services. Some of the vendors and applications listed in the table provide colleges and universities with off-the-shelf solutions; others are potential competitors or strategic partners. Researching this ever-changing list of vendors and applications, comparing solutions to home-grown or go-it-alone options, selecting the appropriate approach, implementing these solutions, managing these relationships, and maintaining institution-wide technology standards and architectures will require the devotion of time and attention to ensure colleges and universities are identifying the right solution.

Table 6.1. E-Business and Vendor Applications in the Market

Process Area	Sample of E-Business Vendors
On-line admission applications	Embark, CollegeNet, XAP
On-line student services	Campus Pipeline, MyBytes.com, Jenzabar
On-line textbooks	varsitybooks.com, textbooks.com, ecampus.com, efollet.com
On-line procurement	CommerceOne, Ariba
On-line alumni communities, contributions, and merchandising	Alumniconnections.com (from Harris Publications)
Tools and systems for on-line delivery and management	Blackboard, Centra, Convene, eCollege.com, WebCT, Eduprise.com
On-line content distributors	Caliber, UNEXT.com, Pensare
Learning portals	Asymetrix's click2learn.com, HungryMinds.com, Ziff-Davis's SmartPlanet.com, Blackboard.com

Process, Organization, and Policies

The promises of reengineering remain unrealized for many institutions. In many instances, large, expensive programs designed to institute change have been only partially implemented, often with less-than-expected results. As a result, it is likely that few fret the passing of the reengineering trend. Many institutions, however, have replaced these process improvement projects with still larger (and order-of-magnitude more expensive) enterprise systems implementations. (These implementations are often referred to as ERP implementations, for their enterprise resource planning approach to integrating student, financial, and human resources systems.) In this context, the influx of e-business projects or initiatives may be welcomed with less than open arms due partially to fatigue from these previous efforts. Conversely, others may be eager to embrace an e-business strategy as the vehicle to achieve organizational restructuring with more tangible and expeditious results.

The implementation of e-business applications, similar to reengineering and ERP projects, will require process redesign, organization restructuring and alignment, new job descriptions, and review and revision of policies. Thus, they will be met with similar skepticism and resistance and necessitate institution-wide change management strategies to ensure success. The enabler may have changed—in this case, Internet-based applications—but these projects will require institutions to continue the difficult and often arduous restructuring efforts. Institutions that have realized significant progress from previous efforts will be able to leverage these initiatives and should experience a higher probability of success.

Academic policies too will require reexamination. Policies and processes related to articulation, faculty evaluation, faculty development, and assessment of student outcomes, among many others, will require review and revision by institutions that expect to succeed in the delivery of on-line courses, programs, and supporting services. (See Chapter Five for a detailed discussion of integrated information policy to support e-business.)

Tax, Legal, and Security Issues

Although there are similarities with previous institutional improvement efforts, new challenges exist as well. Implementing e-business applications will require institutions to examine tax, legal, and security issues. In the area of tax and legal issues, institutions will be forced to examine intellectual property issues, review Internet-based revenues for unrelated business income tax (UBIT), and document legal and audit trails. Security issues, while examined in ERP implementations, will be heightened in importance since vendors and other constituents will have expanded access to institutional data and systems requiring firewalls, authentication, encryption, confidentiality and integrity controls, and enhanced management of security breaches. These issues elevate risk management challenges to the top of the agenda of senior management at all colleges and universities. (See Chapter Four for a detailed discussion of the technical building blocks needed to address these challenges.)

Integrating Information Management

Colleges and universities, like other organizations, have struggled to integrate information management. Replacing formerly disparate systems and applications to improve decision-making capabilities and minimize shadow systems and resultant redundant data entry and maintenance was the key impetus for many institutions to implement ERP solutions. Examples of unintegrated systems—student systems that were unable to share data with general ledger, human resources, advancement, and grants and contracts systems—were commonplace throughout many, if not most, colleges and universities.

E-business applications will once again highlight the need for integrated systems. Without seamless interfaces to administrative systems from Web-based applications, the processes of colleges and universities will once again require redundant data entry, confound data integrity, and hamper decision making.

The simplest example concerns on-line admissions applications. Many institutions provide this functionality today. However, many also require manual data entry into the institution's admission systems of information previously input into the Web application (due to the lack of an interface between the two). The process is convenient for students but more expensive to administer than one in which paper-based applications are used.

The key technology issue for application integration is how to get applications that are based on different technologies and with differing business processes and data models to work together in a common way on a network. More specifically, how does an organization integrate an e-business application—whether a distance-learning course management system, an on-line student services application, a procurement application, or others—on top of what already exists? How is integration accomplished quickly with minimal disruption to everyday operations, not to mention preexisting investment? The solutions, neither trivial nor inexpensive, are crucial for scaling e-business functionality. In general, integration methods that provide the highest level of functionality and the greatest degree of transparency also are the most complex to implement.

It is not surprising that a significant portion of the growth for software and services to support electronic business—expected to skyrocket from $25 billion in 1998 to $104 billion in 2003 in the United States (Input, 1999)—is attributed to systems-integration projects that link companies' Web sites to administrative systems. It is expected that this trend is applicable to higher education as well.

Framework for an E-Business Strategy

At PricewaterhouseCoopers, we have identified four evolutionary stages for adopting an e-business strategy relevant for all industries, including higher education: presence, integration, transformation, and convergence (see Figure 6.1).

Presence

The first step to doing business on the Internet is to establish a presence there. Often called "electronic brochureware," this presence usually describes your institution's basic programs, courses, and services, and gives contact information. Examples include on-line descriptions of purchasing procedures, on-line catalogues of campus information, and on-line syllabi and course information. At this stage, risks are small, and so are the likely bottom-line benefits. Nonetheless, this is an essential stage for experimenting, learning, and building commitment. Virtually all colleges and universities have reached this first stage because it is relatively simple to create and maintain a read-only file of programs, courses, and faculty for interested parties.

Figure 6.1. Evolutionary Stages for Adopting an E-Business Strategy

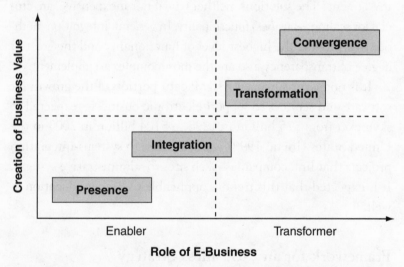

Source: PricewaterhouseCoopers LLP. Copyright © 1999 Pricewaterhouse-Coopers LLP.

Integration

In the integration stage, an institution connects with its wider network of suppliers and students by extending its reach beyond institutional walls. At this stage, your institution will enable business functions through the Web—for example, by allowing students to register for courses on-line. In addition, you will use business-to-business links with procurement vendors, the Department of Education (for financial aid eligibility verification), funding agencies, research subcontractors, benefit administration vendors, and financial institutions.

Opportunities exist at this stage to realize efficiency and revolutionize customer service. However, challenges exist to integrate Web-based applications with legacy administrative information systems, provide prompt customer service, compete with nimble new entrants, and allocate resources to significant IT investments. Also, tax, legal, risk management, and audit issues loom larger as you begin to conduct real business on-line.

Typically in this stage, colleges and universities do the following:

- *Begin offering on-line courses.* The institution will experiment with technology-enabled and -mediated courses to test and improve processes for the development and delivery of on-line courses. The objectives will be to generate additional revenues, stay ahead of competitors, and gain feedback in an operational setting to test assumptions and help refine new process, organization, and technology designs prior to full-scale implementation.

- *Provide on-line student services.* Students will be able to go on-line to apply for admissions and financial aid, register for courses, monitor progress, check financial status and pay bills, select housing options, and e-mail faculty. Many institutions use packaged applications such as Campus Pipeline, MyBytes.com, or vendor-provided ERP system enhancements.

- *Provide on-line alumni and development services.* Web-based applications enable on-line pledge processing, payment processing (with an instantaneous e-mail receipt for acknowledgements), record updating, event registration and reply, and membership sign-up and renewal.

- *Transform the procurement cycle.* On-line market sites will dominate procurement, streamlining request-for-proposal processes and ordering and payment procedures. Procurement processes will be radically shortened, thereby reducing costs amid plentiful choices and more and better services. For a majority of purchases, staff and faculty will order directly from a Web-based market site that is integrated with the administrative system of the institution and the vendor. Information regarding established contracts—products, prices, usage, and so forth—will be immediately accessible and verifiable.

- *Develop intricate links throughout the entire research administration process.* Research-intensive colleges and universities will seamlessly share information with principal investigators, funding agencies, corporations (funding research and establishing technology transfer arrangements), clinical trial sites, subcontractors, and other constituents. This process will reduce costs, shorten cycle time, improve service, and become a required core competency for competing for federal and industry research dollars.

Transformation

Process specialization and disaggregation of the value chain drive the transformation stage. With the e-business infrastructure in place, executives can focus on the job of delineating their core and non-core competencies. E-business allows institutions to unbundle operations more easily, retaining only those components of the value chain where a competitive advantage exists.

An institution in the industry transformation stage will outsource many of its noncore activities. Opportunities exist for your institution to identify and invest in activities that truly add value, exploit process excellence by selling to others, rebundle products and services, and create new entry barriers by developing superior knowledge of customer needs and wants. However, challenges exist since margins are squeezed and new entrants increase competition. And identifying and partnering with the best vendors may be impeded ultimately if the best vendors form exclusive arrangements with other institutions, leaving some institutions to choose among less-than-optimal partners.

It is expected that at this stage, colleges and universities will do the following:

- *Form strategic partnerships with vendors to complement expertise and resources.* Although some institutions will develop and provide on-line services themselves, most institutions will select a partner for on-line procurement, student services, research administration, advancement, and distance learning. This disaggregation of the value chain will be met with some controversy and resistance on the part of various stakeholders, but the results—reduced costs, improved services, and heightened focus on core competencies—will prove beneficial to the higher education industry generally and to individual colleges and universities specifically. Narrowing margins and increasing competition will force even reluctant institutions to outsource many noncore processes.

- *Develop a core competency in technology-mediated delivery of education.* In many instances, distance education courses and programs will be developed and delivered by a separate organization (perhaps a for-profit entity in the form of a university.com subsidiary such as New York University, Columbia University, and the University of Nebraska have already done), freed from the confines of the traditional institution but supporting the institution-wide mission. Asynchronous options will allow students, not colleges, to determine the convenient time, place, and pace for education, ideal for lifelong learning. Students will be able to choose modules from a variety of providers, thereby enhancing consumer choice but intensifying competition. (See Chapter Three for a detailed discussion of the changing relationships between providers and learners prompted by e-learning.)

Convergence

The fourth and final stage, convergence is about more than just the much-heralded coming together of consumer electronics, information technology, telecommunications, and e-business. Convergence leads to the blurring of market boundaries. For example, colleges and universities will soon be competing with training providers, publishers, software vendors, and entertainment providers as these industries converge into the learning industry.

Certainly opportunities exist to enter new markets with no baggage, exploit process skills (for example, superior customer skills), and exploit strong brand name, but challenges exist on how to maintain entry barriers for core businesses (that is, teaching and research) and where to focus the brand name. Colleges and universities will find themselves competing across industries and geography against the University of Phoenix, UNEXT.com, Harcourt Direct Learning, the Open University, and even the likes of Thomson Learning, Asymetrix, Microsoft U, and a multitude of accredited corporate universities.

Strategies for the Future

These opportunities presented by e-business preclude the option of waiting for the technologies to mature and the implications to become discernible and lucid. The rising popularity of the Internet, increasingly demanding customers and unrelenting expectations for expedited services, continuing cost constraints, and emerging opportunities for new revenues will compel colleges and universities to adopt an e-business strategy. Institutions with a carefully constructed plan that considers institution-wide implications will substantially benefit from this transition. Others will be left to struggle and fret over why, where, how, and when to move into e-business, placing them at a competitive disadvantage for students, research grants, and contributions, in addition to hampering efforts to increase the effectiveness and efficiency of administrative processes.

To navigate the stages of an e-business strategy successfully, institutions must do more than just enable on-line transactions over the Web. Assessing your institution's readiness or developing a strategic plan for e-business must include an examination of a multitude of capabilities, not just an evaluation of the campus Web site. The multifaceted challenges that must be confronted to succeed in e-business span the entire institution, necessitating close coordination and dependencies among disparate organizational entities. This is the true challenge of doing e-business.

At PricewaterhouseCoopers, we have identified eight areas in which preparedness is vital to exploit the opportunities presented by e-business (see Figure 6.2):

- E-business strategy
- Organization and capabilities
- Delivery and operations
- Processes
- Systems and technology
- Performance management
- Security
- Tax and legal

In each of the eight areas, you will need to assess your institution's preparedness, identify gaps, and develop plans to optimize your institution's readiness and improve its ability to provide Internet-enabled services. (The chapter appendix contains a diagnostic process to help with this assessment.) Assessment of these categories can serve as an initial gauge of your institution's e-business readiness. In essence, such a diagnosis determines where your institution is deficient in its preparedness. Armed with this information, your institution will be sufficiently well informed to develop a strategic plan for e-business and a corresponding implementation plan, significantly improving the likelihood of success in the increasingly complex and competitive world of e-business.

Lessons Learned

In developing this strategic plan for e-business, your institution should leverage its own experience and that of others in the higher education industry. Other industries such as financial services and

Figure 6.2. Eight Areas of Preparedness for E-Business

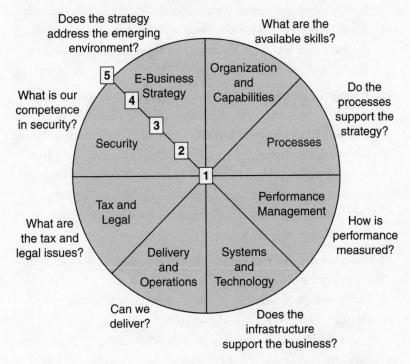

Source: PricewaterhouseCoopers LLP. Copyright © 1999 Pricewaterhouse-Coopers LLP.

retail companies (for example, e*Trade, Dell, Schwab, and Amazon.com) offer insights on the development and deployment of successful e-business strategies.

Based on our experiences, we have identified five key lessons learned that higher education institutions should incorporate into their strategic planning process:

1. *Link e-business objectives to critical business issues.* Your rationale for e-business should be aligned with your institutional mission, strategies, and priorities. Simply put, "e-business"

will become all business. If your institution's strategic objectives are to raise academic quality, reduce costs, increase student quality, or improve student service, e-business initiatives should be undertaken in support of those institution-wide strategic objectives.

2. *Focus on e-business as a business-driven project.* E-business is more than a technology initiative; its impact will be pervasive and should be viewed as a mission-critical undertaking. Brand issues are paramount. Accordingly, the project sponsorship for an e-business project should emanate from the president, provost, or executive vice president's office to ensure that sufficient importance and institution-wide perspective are embedded in this endeavor.

3. *Acknowledge that culture and change are more complicated than the technology.* Once you have determined your e-business objectives (aligned as appropriate with your institution's strategic objectives) and designed the undertaking as a business-driven project, developing an effective change management plan is the next critical activity. Instituting the technology—the infrastructure, applications, or interfaces—is relatively straightforward, although resource intensive. Processes, policies, and organization will likely undergo a transformation. To do so effectively requires a formal change management plan replete with frequent communication of key messages to a variety of constituents.

4. *Do not treat e-business as just a way to communicate with customers; it will change the way you operate.* If you view e-business as simply an interface, you will miss transformation opportunities. E-business is more than just enabling on-line transactions. It will lead to the substitution of network-based technologies and processes for physical locations, manual processes, or other expediting functions that necessitate human attention or increase costs but do not add actual

value. These technologies transform an institution by altering customer service models, enabling personalization of services, providing services at any time, and establishing new relationships with suppliers and other key constituents.

5. *Ensure that business units take ownership, but make sure that central leadership, coordination, and development are also priorities.* In colleges and universities, it is likely that the admissions office has initiated discussion with on-line admissions application vendors, the registrar has spoken with Campus Pipeline or a similar vendor, the directors of purchasing and accounts payable are intrigued by Commerce One's solution, and the advancement office is considering Harris On-line. Although initiative at the business unit level is necessary, unmanaged activities will ultimately distract institutional focus and resources. These individual process-specific decisions must be made only after carefully considering institution-wide objectives and priorities.

Conclusion

Is your institution ready for the widespread adoption of e-commerce applications and the institution-wide transition to e-business? E-business has already begun to and will continue to alter dramatically all industries, including the higher education industry and individual colleges and universities. Reengineering and ERP initiatives will continue unfettered, incorporating the functionality that is now available on-line. Strategic partnerships increasingly will be used, further disaggregating the value chain and redefining the roles of colleges and universities.

As institutions successfully navigate the stages of e-business—from presence to integration to transformation and, finally, to convergence—substantial opportunities will become available for students, faculty, staff, alumni, and other constituents. Benefits will include improved and expedited services, reduced cycle time, increased process efficiencies, improved decision making, expanded access for students, alleviated capacity constraints, personalized and customized marketing opportunities, and expanded market opportunities. But threats will loom large, because failure to provide e-business functionality will result in competitive disadvantages for institutions. If institutions are unable to connect key constituents and provide on-line services easily, someone else will be ready, able, and eager to do so.

Appendix: A Diagnostic Approach to Assessing Your Campus's Readiness for E-Business

In each of the eight areas below, you will need to assess your institution's preparedness, identify gaps, and develop plans to optimize readiness and improve your institution's ability to provide Internet-enabled services. The following categories and related questions can serve as an initial gauge of your institution's e-business readiness. The set of questions to be answered depends on the e-business initiative; for example, distance education strategies generate different risk issues than do e-procurement strategies, and enabling student services on the Web presents yet another set of issues. These questions must be tailored to the situation at hand.

In essence, such a diagnosis will determine where your institution is deficient in its preparedness. Armed with this information, your institution will be sufficiently well informed to develop a strategic plan and corresponding implementation plan, significantly increasing the likelihood of success in the increasingly complex and competitive world of e-business.

E-Business Strategy

E-business strategy means more than just determining target markets and developing business plans describing the return on investment. It is a comprehensive view of your institution's e-business goals, expected outcomes, rationale, branding, marketing, and launch strategy.

The following sample diagnostic questions assess readiness:

- Do you have an electronic business strategy?
- Do key stakeholders buy in to the plan?
- Have you clearly defined the goal of your e-business strategy?
- Do you have a robust implementation plan for this strategy, including key milestones?
- Have you created a feedback loop and a time at which you will review the results and reevaluate the strategy? (Market conditions may change and may negate your strategy.)
- Have you developed strategic alliances or partnerships with any vendors for Web-based applications?
- Have you determined the return on investment of your strategy? Have you defined success and set clear milestones to gauge progress and considered your exit strategy should market conditions change?
- Have you developed your funding plan? Do you have a plan to recoup your initial investment?
- Have you developed your strategy based on information from current and prospective users? Are you building sites that meet their needs?
- Have you developed a brand for your institution and a corresponding process to maintain, protect, and strengthen this key asset?
- Have you developed a promotional campaign for your Web strategy?
- Have you adequately identified the downside risks? Do you have a plan to address them?

Organization and Capabilities

E-business is far more than putting up a Web site and creating on-line processes. Each unit that implements e-business requires dramatic change. Often referred to as e-engineering, e-business means that organization structures change, new positions are created, roles and responsibilities are altered dramatically, and new ventures are launched. For many institutions, requisite skills are in short supply, and outsourcing arrangements are used to accelerate the transition to a new way of doing business.

The following sample diagnostic questions assess readiness:

- Do you have clearly identified business leaders and administrators responsible for e-business?
- Are the appropriate people in the organization responsible for electronic commerce?
- Have you appointed Web designers responsible for the appearance of your Internet applications?
- Have you communicated e-business roles and responsibilities across the entire institution?
- Can you be as entrepreneurial as you need to be?
- Can you move rapidly enough to achieve your goals within your stated time line?
- Have you appointed Web architects whose roles are to turn business requirements into a system design, capabilities for on-line transaction processing (for students, principle investigators, alumni, and vendors), and related services?
- Does the organization have access to appropriately qualified resources?
- Do you have a plan to retrain staff?
- Have you rethought your human resources performance and reward systems?

Delivery and Operations

The IT support area in your organization will go through its own transformation as it supports your e-business initiatives. And not only will the roles of your IT professionals change, but new organizations will need to be developed to take on new quasi-IT tasks, such as converting content to on-line formats. This area includes the following topics: backup and continuity planning, development of new content, content management, managing service providers, preventing systems failure, systems maintenance, Web site development and implementation, database administration, interfaces and messaging, network management, and service management.

The following sample diagnostic questions assess readiness:

- Have you put in place a process for creation, publication, evaluation, and quality assurance of all Web content on an ongoing basis?

- Have you defined a uniform set of Web design principles for use across the institution that have been communicated to all schools, divisions, and departments and are used by all Web applications?

- Has your institution put in place backup systems that automatically allow access to your Web site should the primary system fail?

Processes

E-business means e-engineering your processes. You cannot simply put your existing forms on-line. To take full advantage of the promise of Web-enabling existing processes, the underlying process must be completely rethought and dramatically changed. Linkages among existing systems need to be developed, support desks need to be implemented, upgrades need to be planned and executed, and controls need to be in place.

The following sample diagnostic questions assess readiness:

- If you plan to offer full programs (degree or nondegree) over the Internet, do you have the supporting processes in place?

- Has your institution developed Web-based applications to provide enabled services and transactions over the Internet (for example, on-line applications, on-line registration, and on-line alumni pledges)? If so, have you developed the plan to change the process?

- Have you linked your new processes to your existing systems? Do these Internet-based applications feed data directly into your core administration (for example, student, financials, human resources, research, or advancement) without manual intervention?

- Do you have on-line links with suppliers for functions such as ordering goods and services, remitting payment, and submission of proposals or quotes?
- Do you use off-line methods to promote your Web site?
- Do you offer a customer help line that is available twenty-four hours a day, seven days a week, to assist customers with technical problems encountered while using your Web-based applications?

Systems and Technology

E-business depends on adequate systems and technology infrastructure to support your objectives. The systems and technology area includes back-end systems, front-end systems, middleware, and transaction processing, as well as an overarching IT strategic plan to update capabilities continually to meet your e-business requirements.

The following sample diagnostic questions assess readiness:

- Does your institution use accepted Internet standards for both internal and external systems?
- Have you assessed the current suitability of IT technical resources for e-business?
- Has your institution implemented automatic systems to check the consistency and quality of Web sites?
- Are the technologies being used to support e-commerce suitable and scalable?
- Are the current electronic delivery channels appropriate based on user preferences?
- Is the organization able to respond to and capitalize on rapid changes in underlying technologies and delivery channels?
- Are the e-commerce services implemented to minimize additional investment and duplicated business logic?

Performance Management

You will need to establish and monitor tailored criteria by which to judge e-business effectiveness and to manage and improve your e-business initiatives. These should be linked to institutional objectives and priorities. Measures can be strategic (for example, student satisfaction, impact on learning outcomes, impact on research productivity), financial (for example, revenues generated, impact on process costs), or transactional (for example, Web site availability, user profile and usage).

The following sample diagnostic questions assess readiness:

- Have you already considered how you will monitor the success of your Internet-based services and functionality (for example, improved services, increased enrollments, reduced costs, reduced queues or cycle time for registration and other transactions, increased revenues)?

- Do you have a plan to collect and analyze information and data regularly (for example, feedback from students and business partners, press coverage, traffic, matching of achievements with original objectives of the Web site, improved communication with all stakeholders, and image)?

- From a user perspective, is the e-commerce service providing satisfactory service levels?

- Are service levels and usage monitored on a regular basis?

- Does the organization have in place a means to monitor and report on key performance indicators and the realization of business benefits?

Security

E-business exposes your campus to new security risks: cybercrime, loss of data, and privacy concerns. Identifying and addressing security risks can mitigate these concerns and instill confidence for all of your campus constituents.

The following sample diagnostic questions assess readiness:

- Has your institution appointed a security officer responsible for e-business security?

- Have you established a set of security standards that have been communicated institution-wide?

- Have you implemented some form of authentication (for example, log-on IDs and passwords) to control access to sensitive areas of your Web site?

- Have you created controls (for example, firewalls) to protect the underlying network infrastructure and Internet connections?

- Have e-commerce projects adequately considered and addressed the implementation of security that is appropriate for the e-commerce solution?

- Has the organization taken reasonable steps to minimize the potential for a security breach?

- Have you implemented confidentiality and process integrity controls over your e-business application?

Tax and Legal

Tax and legal issues related to e-business abound. Involving your legal department and soliciting the advice of tax consultants is an important part of planning for e-business. Failure to do so can result in unfortunate and unforeseen circumstances, even stopping a strategy in its tracks.

The following sample diagnostic questions assess readiness:

- If your organization generates any revenue from sales over the Internet, have these revenue sources been reviewed for exposure to unrelated business income tax (UBIT)?

- If your organization receives fees for providing any type of services over the Internet (such as Internet access, e-mail, or search services), have these activities been reviewed for exposure to UBIT?

- If your organization has any publications that appear on-line that include any type of advertising (such as advertisements, placards, running banners, and so forth), have these activities been reviewed for potential exposure to UBIT?

- If your organization's Web site has a chat room where users can participate in electronic discussions, are discussions monitored for content that could jeopardize your tax-exempt status, such as the endorsement of political candidates?

- Does the e-commerce system keep adequate legal and audit trails to support e-commerce transactions?

- Has a policy on intellectual property been developed that stipulates ownership of content and revenue sharing procedures?

How to Use This Diagnostic Tool

To use this diagnostic tool effectively, your institution must undertake the following activities:

1. Answer questions honestly by involving relevant constituents
2. Identify gaps in e-business readiness (based on questions to which the answers are no)
3. Determine the root causes of the identified deficiencies
4. Develop a plan and timetable to address deficiencies based on institution-wide objectives and internal capabilities

Achieving the promises of e-business requires successful navigation of a multitude of challenges. The pervasiveness of these challenges necessitates an institution-wide approach to assessing e-business readiness, identifying deficiencies, developing a strategic plan, and proceeding with implementation.

References

Input. "U.S. Systems Integration Market 1998–2003."
[www.input.com/about_input.htm]. 1999.

Moretti, C., and Johnston, P. *Worldwide IT Training and Education Markets and Trends*. Framingham, Mass.: International Data Corporation, 1998. [www.idc.com].

Porter, M. E. *Competitive Advantage: Creating and Sustaining Superior Performance*. New York: Free Press, 1985.

Index